I0016029

Cybersecurity for Beginners

A Comprehensive Guide on Protecting Against Digital Threats in the Modern World

Liam Peterson

© **Copyright 2024 - All rights reserved.**

No portion of this book may be reproduced in any form without written permission from the publisher or author, except as permitted by U.S. copyright law.

Legal Notice:
This book is copyright protected. This is only for personal use. You cannot amend, distribute, sell, use, quote or paraphrase any part or the content within this book without the consent of the author.

Disclaimer Notice:

This publication is designed to provide accurate and authoritative information in regard to the subject matter covered. It is sold with the understanding that neither the author nor the publisher is engaged in rendering legal, investment, accounting or other professional services. While the publisher and author have used their best efforts in preparing this book, they make no representations or warranties with respect to the accuracy or completeness of the contents of this book and specifically disclaim any implied warranties of merchantability or fitness for a particular purpose. No warranty may be created or extended by sales representatives or written sales materials. The advice and strategies contained herein may not be suitable for your situation. You should consult with a professional when appropriate. Neither the publisher nor the author shall be liable for any loss of profit or any other commercial damages, including but not limited to special, incidental, consequential, personal, or other damages.

Table of Contents

Introduction

In the digital age, the term 'cybersecurity' has become a staple in both technical and non-technical conversations. At its core, cybersecurity refers to the practice of protecting systems, networks, and programs from digital attacks. These cyberattacks are usually aimed at accessing, changing, or destroying sensitive information; extorting money from users; or interrupting normal business processes.

Initially, cybersecurity was a concern primarily for large corporations and governments. However, the evolution of the internet and digital technology has expanded its relevance to every individual and business. In today's interconnected world, everyone, from individuals to small businesses to multinational corporations, is a potential target for cyberattacks.

The scope of cybersecurity has broadened to encompass a variety of areas including, but not limited to, network security, information security, operational security, application security, end-user education, and disaster recovery/business continuity planning. This diversification is a direct response to the varying nature of threats faced in different domains. For instance, network security focuses on protecting the integrity of a network from intrusions, whereas information security is about safeguarding the confidentiality and integrity of data.

So, why is this important today?

Protection Against Data Breaches and Attacks: In an era where data has become one of the most valuable commodities, cybersecurity plays a crucial role in protecting personal and organizational data from unauthorized access and cyberattacks. Data breaches can lead to significant financial losses and damage to reputation.

Maintaining Privacy and Confidentiality: Cybersecurity is essential in maintaining the privacy of individuals and organizations. In the face of threats like identity theft and ransomware, effective cybersecurity measures are vital in keeping sensitive information confidential.

Ensuring Business Continuity: For businesses, cybersecurity is integral to their continuity. Cyberattacks can disrupt operations and lead to substantial downtime, impacting revenue and trust.

Compliance with Regulatory Requirements: Many industries are subject to regulatory requirements regarding data protection and privacy. Cybersecurity ensures compliance with these laws, thus avoiding legal consequences and fines.

Building Trust: In the digital economy, trust is a currency. Robust cybersecurity practices help build trust with customers and stakeholders, assuring them that their data and transactions are secure.

The Dynamic Nature of Cyber Threats

One of the biggest challenges in cybersecurity is the ever-evolving nature of security risks. As technology advances, so do the tactics and techniques of cyber attackers. This necessitates a proactive and adaptive approach to cybersecurity, involving continuous learning and evolving strategies.

For example, with the advent of cloud computing and the Internet of Things (IoT), the attack surface has expanded dramatically, introducing new vulnerabilities. Cybersecurity strategies must, therefore, be dynamic and responsive to these changing technologies and threats.

Cybersecurity is not just the responsibility of IT professionals. In the interconnected world of the internet, everyone has a role to play in cybersecurity. End-user education and awareness are critical in mitigating cyber risks. Simple practices like using strong passwords, being wary of suspicious emails, and keeping software up-to-date can significantly reduce the likelihood of a successful cyberattack.

Evolution of Cyber Threats

The digital world has evolved dramatically over the last few decades, and with it, the nature and sophistication of cyber threats have also transformed. Understanding the historical evolution of these threats provides crucial insights into the challenges faced in cybersecurity today.

The concept of cybersecurity became relevant with the advent of the early computer systems in the 1970s and

1980s. During this era, the first recorded cyber threat was the 'Creeper' virus, which appeared in the early 1970s. It was a self-replicating program that moved across ARPANET (the precursor to the modern internet), displaying a simple message: "I'm the creeper, catch me if you can!" This was followed by the appearance of the first computer worm, known as the 'Morris Worm', in 1988, which slowed down thousands of computers and highlighted the need for better network security protocols.

The 1990s saw the rapid expansion of the internet, bringing with it an increase in the prevalence and sophistication of cyber threats. This era marked the emergence of malware – software designed to disrupt, damage, or gain unauthorized access to computer systems. Notable examples from this period include the 'Melissa' virus and the 'ILOVEYOU' worm, which caused widespread damage and highlighted the vulnerabilities in email systems and the need for better email security practices.

With the dawn of the 21st century, cyber threats became more than just a nuisance; they evolved into a tool for significant financial crime and espionage. The 2000s witnessed the emergence of cybercrime with activities such as identity theft, phishing scams, and the proliferation of spyware. This era also saw the rise of botnets, networks of infected computers used to carry out attacks, and the beginning of Distributed Denial of Service (DDoS) attacks, which targeted major websites and online services.

The 2010s were characterized by the involvement of state-sponsored groups in cyber attacks, marking a shift from cybercrime to cyber warfare. The discovery of the 'Stuxnet' worm in 2010, a sophisticated piece of malware allegedly developed by a nation-state to sabotage Iran's nuclear program, demonstrated how cyber attacks could have real-world consequences. This era also saw the rise of Advanced Persistent Threats (APTs) – long-term targeted attacks where attackers infiltrate a network and remain undetected for extended periods.

The current landscape of cyber threats is dominated by ransomware attacks, where attackers encrypt an organization's data and demand a ransom for its release. The widespread impact of ransomware attacks, such as the 'WannaCry' and 'NotPetya' attacks in 2017, highlighted the vulnerabilities in outdated systems and the importance of regular software updates. Additionally, the integration of artificial intelligence and machine learning in cyber attacks has introduced a new level of sophistication and automation, making detection and prevention more challenging.

The history of cyber threats is a testament to their ever-evolving nature. Each advancement in technology brings new security challenges. The rise of cloud computing, the Internet of Things (IoT), and mobile technology has expanded the attack surface and introduced new vulnerabilities. Cybercriminals continue to exploit these vulnerabilities, making cybersecurity a continuously evolving field.

Basic Terminology

Basic terminology is important for understanding the threats, technologies, and strategies that form the foundation of this field. So let's go.

Malware

Malware, short for malicious software, is a broad term that encompasses any software intentionally designed to cause damage to a computer, server, client, or computer network. Types of malware include viruses, worms, Trojan horses, ransomware, and spyware.

Virus

A virus is a type of malware that, when executed, replicates itself by modifying other computer programs and inserting its own code. Viruses often spread to other computers and networks when these infected programs are transferred.

Worm

A worm is a standalone malware that replicates itself in order to spread to other computers. Unlike a virus, it does not need to attach itself to an existing program. Worms often exploit vulnerabilities in operating systems or other software to spread without user interaction.

Trojan Horse

A Trojan horse, or Trojan, is a type of malware that disguises itself as a legitimate file or software to trick users into loading and executing the malware on their systems. Unlike viruses and worms, Trojans do not self-replicate.

Ransomware

Ransomware is a form of malware that encrypts the victim's files, with the attacker demanding a ransom from the victim to restore access to the data upon payment.

Spyware

Spyware is a type of malware that gathers information about a person or organization without their knowledge, often leading to privacy breaches.

Phishing

Phishing is a cyber attack that uses disguised email as a weapon. The goal is to trick the email recipient into believing that the message is something they want or need — a request from their bank, for instance, or a note from someone in their company — and to click a link or download an attachment.

Firewall

A firewall is a network security device that monitors and controls incoming and outgoing network traffic based on predetermined security rules. It establishes a barrier between a trusted internal network and untrusted external networks.

Encryption

Encryption is a process of converting information or data into a code to prevent unauthorized access. It's a critical way to secure data, particularly during transmission or while it's stored on networks and systems outside of one's physical control.

VPN (Virtual Private Network)

A VPN extends a private network across a public network and enables users to send and receive data across shared or public networks as if their computing devices were directly connected to the private network.

Two-Factor Authentication (2FA)

Two-Factor Authentication, often referred to as 2FA, is an extra layer of security used to ensure the security of online accounts beyond just a username and password.

DDoS Attack (Distributed Denial of Service)

A DDoS Attack is a malicious attempt to disrupt the normal traffic of a targeted server, service, or network by overwhelming the target or its surrounding infrastructure with a flood of Internet traffic.

Botnet

A botnet is a number of Internet-connected devices, each of which is running one or more bots. Botnets can be used to perform DDoS attacks, steal data, send spam, and allow the attacker access to the device and its connection.

Cybersecurity

Cybersecurity refers to the practice of defending computers, servers, mobile devices, electronic systems, networks, and data from malicious attacks.

Hacker

A hacker is a person who uses computers to gain unauthorized access to data. Hackers can be classified based on their intent: white hat (ethical hacking), black hat (criminal or malicious hacking), and grey hat (a blend of both ethical and malicious hacking).

Cybersecurity for Individuals and Organizations

In an era where digital technology permeates every aspect of our lives, cybersecurity has become a paramount concern not just for organizations but also for individuals.

Cybersecurity for Individuals

Protecting Personal Information: Individuals store a vast amount of personal information online. From social security numbers to bank details, cyber threats pose a risk of identity theft and financial fraud. Effective cybersecurity measures help protect this sensitive information from unauthorized access and exploitation.

Safeguarding Privacy: With the rise of social media and online platforms, personal privacy is increasingly vulnerable. Cybersecurity helps in safeguarding personal photos, communications, and data from being compromised and misused.

Ensuring Online Safety: Individuals, especially minors, can be susceptible to cyberbullying, stalking, and other forms of online harassment. Cybersecurity tools and awareness are crucial in protecting against these digital threats.

Building Digital Trust: As more transactions and interactions happen online, the assurance of security is vital for maintaining trust in digital services. Strong cybersecurity measures build confidence in the use of online services for shopping, banking, and communication.

Educating and Empowering Users: Cybersecurity is not just about tools and technologies; it's also about educating individuals on safe online practices. Knowledge of cybersecurity principles empowers users to navigate the digital world securely.

Cybersecurity for Organizations

Protecting Sensitive Data: Organizations, whether big or small, handle sensitive data, including customer information, intellectual property, and financial records. Cybersecurity is crucial in protecting this data from breaches that can have legal, financial, and reputational repercussions.

Maintaining Business Continuity: Cyber attacks can cripple an organization's operations, leading to significant downtime and loss of business. A robust cybersecurity framework ensures business continuity by preventing or quickly mitigating cyber attacks.

Complying with Regulatory Requirements: Many industries face strict regulatory requirements for data protection and privacy (like GDPR in Europe). Cybersecurity helps organizations comply with these regulations, avoiding hefty fines and legal consequences.

Building Customer Trust: Customers expect their data to be handled securely. Organizations that demonstrate strong cybersecurity practices can gain customer trust, which is crucial in today's competitive marketplace.

Preventing Industrial Espionage: In a highly competitive business environment, industrial espionage is a real threat. Cybersecurity measures protect sensitive business strategies and intellectual property from competitors.

Cybersecurity is a shared responsibility. Individuals need to be vigilant about their personal cybersecurity practices, such as using strong passwords and being cautious about the information they share online. Organizations, on the other hand, must ensure they have robust security policies, employee training programs, and effective incident response strategies.

Overview of Common Cyber Threats

Understanding the common cyber threats is crucial for developing effective cybersecurity strategies.

Man-in-the-Middle Attacks (MitM)

Man-in-the-Middle Attacks occur when attackers insert themselves into a two-party transaction. After interrupting the traffic, they can filter and steal data. Two common points of entry for MitM attacks are unsecured public Wi-Fi networks and malware-infected devices, where attackers can intercept data being passed between the victim's device and the network.

Denial-of-Service Attacks (DoS)

Denial-of-Service Attacks flood systems, servers, or networks with traffic to exhaust resources and bandwidth. As a result, the system becomes unable to fulfill legitimate requests. Attackers often use multiple compromised devices as sources of attack traffic, known as Distributed Denial-of-Service (DDoS) attacks.

SQL Injection

A SQL Injection occurs when an attacker inserts malicious code into a server that uses SQL and forces the server to reveal information it normally would not. An attacker could carry out a SQL injection simply by submitting malicious code into a vulnerable website search box.

Zero-Day Exploits

A Zero-Day Exploit hits after a network vulnerability is announced but before a patch or solution is implemented. Attackers target the disclosed vulnerability during this window of time. Zero-day vulnerability threat detection requires constant awareness.

Insider Threats

Insider Threats come from people within the organization, such as employees, former employees, contractors, or business associates, who have inside information concerning the organization's security practices, data, and computer systems. The motivation for these attacks could be to commit fraud, espionage, or sabotage.

Advanced Persistent Threats (APT)

An Advanced Persistent Threat is a prolonged and targeted cyberattack in which an intruder gains access to a network and remains undetected for an extended period. APTs are often conducted by nation-states or state-sponsored groups aiming to steal data or surveil targets over a long time.

IoT Threats

The proliferation of Internet of Things (IoT) devices has expanded the threat landscape. Many IoT devices are not built with security in mind and can be easily compromised. Attackers can exploit these devices to gain unauthorized access, steal data, or enlist these devices in botnets to carry out DDoS attacks.

Malware

Malware, short for malicious software, is an umbrella term for any software intentionally designed to cause damage to a computer, server, or computer network. Malware includes viruses, worms, Trojan horses, and ransomware. These malicious programs can steal, encrypt, delete data, alter or hijack core computing functions, and spy on the user's computer activity without their knowledge.

Phishing

Phishing is a cyber attack that uses disguised email as a weapon. The goal is to trick the recipient into believing that the message is something they want or need and to click a link or download an attachment. What really distinguishes phishing is the form the message takes: the attackers masquerade as a trusted entity, often a real or plausibly real person, or a company the victim might do business with.

Ransomware

Ransomware is a type of malware that encrypts a victim's files. The attacker then demands a ransom from the victim to restore access to the data upon payment. Users are shown instructions for how to pay a fee to get the decryption key. The costs can range from a few hundred dollars to thousands, payable to cybercriminals in Bitcoin.

Cyber Threats

First we focuses on three prevalent forms of cyber threats: viruses, malware, and phishing, offering an in-depth analysis of their nature, methods of operation, and potential impact.

Viruses

A virus is a type of malicious software that, when executed, replicates itself by modifying other computer programs and inserting its own code. Designed to spread from host to host, viruses attach themselves to legitimate software programs and files, exploiting their functionality to execute and replicate.

Viruses typically require some form of user action to initiate, such as opening an infected email attachment or downloading a file from a malicious website. Once activated, they can perform a range of malicious activities, including corrupting or deleting data, logging keystrokes, or hijacking core system functions.

The impact of viruses can vary significantly, from harmless pranks to severe data loss, system failure, or compromising sensitive information. Some notorious viruses, like the ILOVEYOU virus, have caused billions of dollars in damages worldwide.

Malware

Malware, short for malicious software, is a broader term that encompasses various forms of harmful software, including viruses, worms, Trojan horses, ransomware, and spyware. Malware is designed to damage, disrupt, or gain unauthorized access to computer systems.

Malware can be spread in numerous ways. For example, worms can replicate and spread independently, while Trojans disguise themselves as legitimate software. Ransomware encrypts data and demands a ransom for its release, and spyware stealthily gathers information without the user's knowledge.

The consequences of malware infections can be extensive, including data theft, financial loss, compromised privacy, and damage to an organization's reputation. In extreme cases, malware like ransomware can cripple entire networks, leading to significant operational disruptions.

Phishing

Phishing is a deceptive technique used by cybercriminals to trick individuals into revealing sensitive information, such as passwords and credit card numbers. It typically involves sending fraudulent communications that appear to come from a reputable source, often via email.

Phishing attacks use social engineering to exploit human psychology. They might imitate emails from trusted entities, like banks or government agencies, urging the recipient to click on a link or open an attachment. These links often lead to fake websites designed to capture sensitive information or install malware on the user's device.

Phishing can lead to various forms of identity theft, financial fraud, and unauthorized access to private networks. It poses a significant threat to individual privacy and security and can compromise the integrity of corporate data.

Anatomy of a Cyber Attack

Let's look at the typical stages of a cyberattack, providing a comprehensive overview of how attackers infiltrate, exploit, and potentially cause damage to systems and networks.

Reconnaissance

Initial Stage: The first phase of a cyber attack involves reconnaissance, where attackers gather information about their target. This can include scanning for vulnerabilities, identifying valuable data, and understanding security protocols. Attackers use various methods such as social engineering, public information, and network scanning to gather this intel.

Objective: The goal in this stage is to create a map of the target's system and identify the easiest points of entry. Attackers look for weaknesses such as outdated software, unsecured networks, and uninformed employees who can be manipulated through social engineering.

Weaponization

Preparation Phase: Once enough information is gathered, attackers move to the weaponization phase. This involves creating or acquiring the tools needed for the attack, such as malware, viruses, or phishing emails. These tools are tailored to exploit the specific vulnerabilities identified during the reconnaissance stage.

Objective: The aim is to create a mechanism to deliver the payload (e.g., malware) effectively to the target system without being detected.

Delivery

Execution Stage: The delivery phase is when the attacker uses various methods to deliver the malicious payload to the target. Common delivery methods include email attachments, compromised websites, or direct network penetration. This stage requires precision to ensure the payload reaches the intended part of the target system.

Objective: The primary goal is to introduce the malicious code into the target's environment without raising suspicion, setting the stage for the next phase of the attack.

Exploitation

Active Attack Phase: Exploitation is the phase where the actual attack takes place. The delivered payload activates and exploits the identified vulnerabilities, allowing the attacker to gain unauthorized access or disrupt services.

Objective: To successfully execute the malicious intent of the payload, whether it's data theft, system damage, or creating a backdoor for future access.

Installation

Establishment Stage: In this stage, attackers establish a foothold within the target's system. The malware or exploit creates a backdoor, allowing attackers to maintain access and avoid detection. This can involve creating hidden pathways, disabling security features, or installing additional malicious software.

Objective: To secure sustained access to the target's network, allowing the attacker to move laterally within the system and reach valuable data or assets.

Command and Control (C2)

Control Phase: The command and control phase involves setting up a system that allows attackers to remotely manipulate the infected systems. This includes sending commands, extracting data, or spreading to other parts of the network.

Objective: To maintain remote control over the compromised systems, facilitating continued exploitation or laying the groundwork for a larger scale attack.

Actions on Objectives

Final Stage: This is where the attacker achieves their primary goal, whether it's data exfiltration, destruction of data, ransomware deployment, or another specific objective. At this point, the attack is fully realized, and the attacker often works to cover their tracks to avoid detection.

Objective: To complete the intended goal of the attack while minimizing the chances of detection and attribution.

Social Engineering and Human Vulnerabilities

In the realm of cybersecurity, technical defenses often receive the most attention. However, human vulnerabilities play a significant role in the security of information systems. Social engineering exploits these human vulnerabilities, often bypassing the most sophisticated technical safeguards.

Social engineering is the art of manipulating people into performing actions or divulging confidential information. Unlike traditional hacking, which exploits technical vulnerabilities, social engineering exploits psychological weaknesses. Common tactics include pretexting (creating a fabricated scenario), phishing (disguised communication, usually email), baiting (offering something enticing), and tailgating (unauthorized physical access).

The primary goal of social engineering is to gain unauthorized access to systems, data, or physical locations, or to compel individuals to act in the attacker's interest.

Human Vulnerabilities in Cybersecurity

1. Trust: Humans are inherently trusting, especially when interacting with someone who appears authoritative or legitimate. Attackers often pose as trusted figures such

as IT support, company executives, or government officials to gain trust and extract sensitive information.

2. Curiosity: Social engineers often exploit people's curiosity through tactics like baiting, where malicious software is hidden within seemingly harmless downloads or email attachments.

3. Fear and Urgency: Creating a sense of urgency or fear is a common technique in social engineering. For instance, phishing emails may warn of a security breach or legal action, pressuring the recipient to act hastily without proper scrutiny.

4. Ignorance and Lack of Awareness: Many users are not aware of the value of the information they possess and how it can be used against them or their organization. Lack of cybersecurity training increases susceptibility to social engineering attacks.

5. Desire to Help: Many social engineering attacks exploit the natural human desire to be helpful. For example, an attacker might pose as a co-worker with an urgent problem that requires immediate access to certain data or systems.

Real-World Examples of Social Engineering

- Phishing Attacks: Phishing is one of the most common forms of social engineering, where attackers send fraudulent emails mimicking legitimate sources to steal data like login credentials and credit card numbers.

- Pretexting Scenarios: In pretexting, attackers create a fabricated scenario to steal information. A classic example is an attacker posing as a bank official to extract personal information from customers.

- Baiting Scenarios: Baiting involves offering something enticing to the victim in exchange for information or access. This could be as simple as a USB drive labeled "confidential" left in a public area.

Mitigating Social Engineering Threats

- Education and Awareness: Regular training and awareness programs are essential to educate employees about social engineering tactics and how to recognize and respond to them.

- Policy and Procedure: Organizations should establish clear policies and procedures for verifying identities and handling sensitive information.

- Encourage Skepticism: Cultivating an environment where it's acceptable to question the legitimacy of unusual requests can significantly reduce the risk of social engineering attacks.

- Regular Security Audits: Conducting regular security audits can help identify potential vulnerabilities in organizational processes that could be exploited through social engineering.

Case Studies of Major Cyber Attacks

The landscape of cybersecurity is punctuated by numerous high-profile cyber attacks that have had significant impacts on individuals, organizations, and even governments. The following is a look at some notable cyberattacks, providing insight into their realization, consequences and lessons learned from them.

The WannaCry Ransomware Attack (2017)

In May 2017, the WannaCry ransomware attack swept across the globe, affecting over 200,000 computers in 150 countries. It targeted computers running the Microsoft Windows operating system by encrypting data and demanding ransom payments in the Bitcoin cryptocurrency.

The attack exploited a vulnerability in Microsoft Windows, specifically in the older versions that had not been updated with recent security patches. The vulnerability was initially discovered by the National Security Agency (NSA) of the United States, but the information was leaked by a group known as the Shadow Brokers.

WannaCry had widespread effects, disrupting operations in many sectors, including healthcare (notably the UK's National Health Service), finance, telecommunications, and more. The total damages were estimated to be in the billions of dollars.

The attack highlighted the importance of regular software updates and patches, the risks associated with hoarding software vulnerabilities, and the need for better cybersecurity awareness and preparedness.

The Equifax Data Breach (2017)

Equifax, one of the largest credit reporting agencies in the US, suffered a massive data breach in 2017, which exposed the personal information of 147 million people.

The breach occurred due to a vulnerability in the Apache Struts web application framework used by Equifax. Despite the availability of a patch for the vulnerability, Equifax had failed to update its systems in time.

The exposed data included names, Social Security numbers, birth dates, addresses, and, in some cases, driver's license numbers. The breach had far-reaching consequences regarding identity theft and fraud for millions of individuals.

This incident underscored the importance of timely software updates and the need for robust security infrastructure and practices, especially for companies handling sensitive personal data.

The Stuxnet Worm (2010)

Stuxnet, discovered in 2010, was a highly sophisticated computer worm that targeted the programmable logic controllers (PLCs) used in industrial control systems. It is widely believed to have been developed by the US and Israeli governments to disrupt Iran's nuclear program.

Stuxnet specifically targeted Siemens Step7 software, exploiting several zero-day vulnerabilities. It was designed to damage centrifuges used in Iran's nuclear enrichment program by causing them to spin out of control while simultaneously showing normal operating readings.

Stuxnet successfully damaged approximately 1,000 centrifuges at Iran's Natanz nuclear facility. The worm marked a significant shift in the landscape of cyber warfare, demonstrating how cyber attacks could have physical, real-world consequences.

Stuxnet highlighted the vulnerabilities in critical infrastructure and the potential of cyber attacks to cause physical damage. It raised global awareness about the need to secure industrial control systems against sophisticated cyber threats.

Emerging Threats in the Cyber World

As technology continues to advance at a rapid pace, new and evolving cyber threats emerge, posing significant challenges to cybersecurity professionals and users alike. This chapter explores some of the emerging threats in the cyber world, their potential impacts, and the challenges they present.

Artificial Intelligence (AI) and Machine Learning (ML) in Cyber Attacks

Overview: The use of AI and ML in cyber attacks is a growing concern. These technologies can be used by attackers to automate complex tasks, such as data analysis and pattern recognition, to identify vulnerabilities and optimize attack strategies.

Impact: AI-driven attacks can be highly effective, adaptive, and difficult to detect. They can accelerate the speed and precision of cyber attacks, making traditional defense mechanisms less effective.

Challenges: Defending against AI-powered threats requires advanced security solutions that can adapt and learn from the evolving tactics of AI-driven malware and attacks.

Internet of Things (IoT) Vulnerabilities

Overview: The proliferation of IoT devices has dramatically expanded the attack surface. Many of these devices lack robust security features, making them vulnerable to cyber attacks.

Impact: Compromised IoT devices can be used for various malicious purposes, including launching distributed denial-of-service (DDoS) attacks, infiltrating networks, and stealing sensitive data.

Challenges: Securing the vast and diverse ecosystem of IoT devices is a significant challenge due to the inconsistency in security standards and the complexity of managing numerous connected devices.

Cloud Security Threats

Overview: With the increasing adoption of cloud computing, cyber threats targeting cloud services and infrastructures are on the rise. These threats exploit vulnerabilities in cloud systems, misconfigurations, and inadequate security practices.

Impact: Attacks on cloud services can lead to data breaches, loss of data integrity, and disruption of services. They also pose risks of data leakage across shared cloud resources.

Challenges: Protecting cloud environments requires a comprehensive approach, including robust encryption, access control, and continuous monitoring for suspicious activities.

Ransomware and Cryptojacking

Overview: Ransomware attacks, which involve encrypting victims' data and demanding a ransom for its release, continue to evolve. Cryptojacking, where attackers use victims' computing resources to mine cryptocurrencies, is also an emerging threat.

Impact: These attacks can cause significant financial losses, disrupt operations, and compromise sensitive data. Cryptojacking also impacts system performance and increases operational costs.

Challenges: Defending against these threats requires robust backup and recovery processes, effective endpoint security, and awareness of the latest ransomware tactics.

Supply Chain and Third-Party Vendor Risks

Overview: Cyber threats targeting supply chains and third-party vendors are becoming more prevalent. Attackers exploit vulnerabilities in the supply chain to gain access to otherwise secure systems.

Impact: These attacks can lead to widespread compromise of multiple organizations through a single point of failure in the supply chain.

Challenges: Ensuring the security of the supply chain involves vetting third-party vendors, implementing stringent security standards, and continuously monitoring for threats.

State-Sponsored Cyber Attacks and Espionage

Overview: State-sponsored cyber attacks and cyber espionage are significant concerns, as nation-states use cyber capabilities to gain strategic advantages, steal intellectual property, and disrupt critical infrastructure.

Impact: Such attacks can have far-reaching political, economic, and social implications, including destabilizing national security and international relations.

Challenges: Defending against state-sponsored attacks requires a coordinated national and international response, along with advanced cybersecurity defenses.

Cybersecurity Principles

The CIA Triad (Confidentiality, Integrity, and Availability) is a central concept in the realm of cybersecurity, providing a structured framework to guide the development of robust security policies. This model, encompassing Confidentiality, Integrity, and Availability, is critical for any organization seeking to protect its information systems effectively.

Confidentiality

Confidentiality is about ensuring that sensitive information is accessed only by authorized individuals. It's crucial for preventing unauthorized disclosure of information, which can lead to severe consequences like privacy breaches and identity theft. To maintain confidentiality, organizations implement strong access control measures such as user authentication and authorization. Encryption plays a key role in protecting data, both at rest and in transit, against unauthorized access. Additionally, classifying data based on sensitivity helps in applying appropriate security measures and controls.

Integrity

Integrity focuses on maintaining the accuracy and consistency of data throughout its lifecycle. This element of the triad is vital for ensuring that information remains unaltered and reliable. Ensuring data integrity involves the use of cryptographic tools like hashing and digital signatures to verify that data has not been altered. Version control systems are crucial in tracking changes and identifying unauthorized modifications. Conducting regular audits and employing intrusion detection systems are also essential practices for maintaining data integrity.

Availability

Availability ensures that information and resources are accessible to authorized users when needed, which is essential for operational efficiency and service continuity. Ensuring availability involves developing redundant systems and failover mechanisms to maintain continuous access. Regular maintenance and system updates are critical in preventing downtime due to system failures or vulnerabilities. Moreover, having a well-developed and tested disaster recovery and business continuity plan is essential for quick restoration of operations after an outage or cyberattack.

Integrating the CIA Triad in Cybersecurity Strategies

The elements of the CIA Triad are interdependent, and a balanced approach to all three is necessary for effective cybersecurity. Overemphasis on one aspect can lead to vulnerabilities in others. For instance, stringent access controls (for confidentiality) might impede the timely availability of data. Conversely, ensuring uninterrupted availability should not come at the cost of compromising data confidentiality or integrity.

Organizations need to integrate the principles of the CIA Triad into their cybersecurity strategies. This involves conducting thorough risk assessments to identify potential threats to confidentiality, integrity, and availability and implementing controls to mitigate these risks. Comprehensive security policies that address all three aspects of the triad are essential, as is ensuring that these policies are effectively communicated and enforced. A layered approach to security is recommended, combining physical, technical, and administrative controls to counter various threats. Additionally, ongoing training and awareness programs are crucial for educating employees about the importance of each element of the triad and equipping them to recognize and respond to potential security threats.

Risk Management in Cybersecurity

Risk management in cybersecurity involves identifying, analyzing, and mitigating risks to an organization's information assets. It's a continuous process aimed at safeguarding data from cyber threats while ensuring the smooth operation of business processes.

Cybersecurity risks refer to potential threats that could exploit vulnerabilities in an organization's information systems, leading to loss or damage of data, financial loss, or damage to the organization's reputation. These risks can originate from various sources, including external threats like hackers and internal threats such as employee errors.

Understanding these risks is the first step in the risk management process. This involves identifying the various assets that need protection, the threats to these assets, and the vulnerabilities that could be exploited.

Risk assessment is a core component of risk management in cybersecurity. It involves evaluating the identified risks to understand their potential impact and likelihood. This evaluation helps in prioritizing the risks based on their severity. A comprehensive risk assessment considers factors like the nature of the data, potential vulnerabilities, the current security measures in place, and the possible outcomes of a security breach.

Developing a Risk Management Strategy

A risk management strategy in cybersecurity is designed to address the identified risks in a way that aligns with the organization's overall objectives and risk appetite. This strategy typically involves a mix of risk mitigation, risk transfer, risk avoidance, and risk acceptance.

1. Risk Mitigation: This involves implementing measures to reduce the likelihood or impact of cybersecurity risks. It includes deploying advanced cybersecurity tools, regular software updates, employee training, and developing strong security policies.

2. Risk Transfer: This involves shifting the risk to a third party, often through insurance or outsourcing certain IT functions to companies with stronger cybersecurity measures.

3. Risk Avoidance: This is the decision to avoid activities that introduce risk. In some cases, this may involve not storing certain types of sensitive data or not engaging in certain business activities.

4. Risk Acceptance: In some instances, the cost of mitigating a risk may outweigh the potential damage. In such cases, an organization may choose to accept the risk, often with contingency plans in place.

Implementing Risk Management Controls

Effective risk management in cybersecurity involves the implementation of various controls. These controls can be classified as technical controls, such as firewalls and encryption; administrative controls, like security policies and employee training; and physical controls, which include secure access to buildings and data centers. The choice of controls depends on the specific risks faced by the organization and the results of the risk assessment process.

Cybersecurity risks are dynamic, constantly evolving with new threats and vulnerabilities. Therefore, continuous monitoring of the security landscape and regular reviews of the risk management strategy are essential. This includes staying updated on the latest cybersecurity threats, regularly reviewing and updating security policies, and conducting periodic security audits.

Risk management in cybersecurity also involves collaboration and information sharing among organizations and cybersecurity experts. Sharing information about threats, vulnerabilities, and risk management strategies can help organizations stay ahead of potential risks.

The Concept of Defense in Depth

Defense in Depth is a strategic approach in cybersecurity, where multiple layers of defense are implemented across an organization's information systems. This concept, drawn from a military strategy, involves creating a multilayered defense mechanism to protect data and information systems from cyber threats. The idea is that if one layer of defense is breached, others will continue to provide protection.

The concept of Defense in Depth originated in military strategy, where it referred to arranging defenses in depth against possible enemy attacks. In cybersecurity, this approach was adopted to provide comprehensive protection against a wide range of cyber threats. The evolution of Defense in Depth reflects the changing nature of cyber threats, from opportunistic viruses to sophisticated, targeted cyber attacks.

Layers of Defense in Depth

Defense in Depth involves multiple layers of security measures, each designed to protect against specific types of threats. These layers encompass both technical and non-technical aspects of security.

- Physical Security: The first layer often involves physical security measures to protect against unauthorized physical access to critical infrastructure, such as data centers and server rooms.

- Network Security: This involves protecting the network infrastructure with firewalls, intrusion detection and prevention systems, and secure network architecture.

- Endpoint Security: Protecting individual devices (endpoints) that connect to the network, such as computers and mobile devices, using antivirus software, anti-malware tools, and device management solutions.

- Application Security: This layer focuses on securing software applications against exploitation, using measures like secure coding practices, application firewalls, and regular vulnerability scanning.

- Data Security: Protecting data through encryption, access controls, and data loss prevention strategies.

- Identity and Access Management (IAM): Controlling who has access to what resources within the organization, using tools like multi-factor authentication and user access controls.

- User Education and Awareness: The human element is a critical layer of defense. Regular training and awareness programs help users recognize and respond appropriately to cyber threats.

Implementing Defense in Depth

Implementing Defense in Depth requires a comprehensive strategy that involves understanding the organization's unique risk profile, the value of its assets, and the potential threats. It also involves:

- Regular Risk Assessments: To identify vulnerabilities and inform the development of a layered defense strategy.

- Strategic Investment in Security Technologies: Allocating resources to the most critical areas of defense.

- Continuous Monitoring and Incident Response: Implementing continuous monitoring to detect and respond to threats in real-time.

- Regular Updates and Patch Management: Keeping all systems and software up to date to protect against known vulnerabilities.

The effectiveness of Defense in Depth lies in its adaptability. As cyber threats evolve, so must the layers of defense. This involves staying informed about the latest threats and trends in cybersecurity and being prepared to adjust strategies and technologies accordingly.

While Defense in Depth is a robust approach, it also presents challenges. These include the complexity of managing multiple layers of security, the need for skilled personnel to implement and maintain these layers, and the potential for increased costs. Additionally, there's a risk of creating a false sense of security if not all layers are effectively managed and updated.

Encryption and Its Importance

Encryption is a fundamental concept in the realm of cybersecurity, serving as a critical tool in protecting data confidentiality and integrity. It involves the conversion of data into a coded form, known as ciphertext, which can only be accessed and understood by those who possess the appropriate decryption key.

Encryption dates back to ancient times when secret messages were written in code to prevent interception by unintended recipients. In the digital age, encryption has become a cornerstone of securing data, whether it's stored on a device or transmitted across networks. The basic principle remains the same: transforming readable data (plaintext) into a format that is unreadable without a specific key (ciphertext).

Types of Encryption

- Symmetric Encryption: This type of encryption uses the same key for both encryption and decryption. It's faster and more efficient, making it suitable for encrypting large volumes of data. However, the key must be shared between the sender and receiver, which can pose a risk if the key is intercepted.

- Asymmetric Encryption: Also known as public-key cryptography, asymmetric encryption uses two keys – a public key for encryption and a private key for decryption. This method allows secure communication without the need to share a private key. However, it's more computationally intensive than symmetric encryption.

The Role of Encryption in Cybersecurity

- Data Confidentiality: Encryption is essential for maintaining data confidentiality. By converting sensitive data into ciphertext, encryption ensures that even if data is intercepted or accessed without authorization, it remains unintelligible and secure.

- Data Integrity: Encryption also plays a role in ensuring data integrity. Certain encryption techniques can detect if data has been altered or tampered with, thereby maintaining its accuracy and reliability.

- Secure Communication: In the context of online communication, encryption is crucial for protecting information transmitted over the internet. From emails to online transactions, encryption safeguards data as it travels across networks.

- Regulatory Compliance: Many regulatory frameworks require the encryption of sensitive data. For example, the General Data Protection Regulation (GDPR) mandates the protection of personal data, for which encryption is a key strategy.

While encryption is a powerful tool for data protection, it presents certain challenges. The management of encryption keys is critical – if keys are lost or compromised, the encrypted data may become irretrievable or vulnerable. Additionally, encryption can introduce complexity into IT systems and requires careful implementation to ensure it doesn't hinder system performance or user experience.

The field of encryption is continuously evolving, especially with advancements in quantum computing. Traditional encryption methods might become vulnerable to quantum computing power, leading to the development of quantum-resistant encryption algorithms. This ongoing evolution underscores the need for continuous research and adaptation in the field of encryption.

Security by Design

Security by Design is a fundamental principle in the development of software and systems, emphasizing the integration of security measures from the earliest stages of design and development, rather than treating it as an afterthought.

The core philosophy of Security by Design is to build security into the DNA of software and systems. This approach entails considering security at every phase of the development process, from initial design to deployment and maintenance. It requires a mindset shift from seeing security as a separate component to an integral part of the entire system architecture and design.

Key Aspects of Security by Design

- Proactive Risk Management: Security by Design involves proactively identifying and mitigating potential security risks during the design phase. This preemptive approach helps in avoiding vulnerabilities that can be exploited in later stages.

- Principle of Least Privilege: This principle involves giving system components only the permissions they need to perform their intended functions, and no more. By limiting access rights, the potential impact of a security breach can be significantly reduced.

- Regular Security Audits and Testing: Continuous testing and auditing are integral to Security by Design. This includes conducting regular code reviews, vulnerability assessments, and penetration testing to identify and address security flaws.

- User-Centric Security: Security by Design also involves considering the user experience in security implementations. This includes designing intuitive security features and user interfaces to ensure that security measures do not hinder usability.

Benefits of Security by Design

- Reduced Vulnerabilities: By considering security from the outset, potential vulnerabilities can be identified and mitigated early, reducing the likelihood of future security breaches.

- Cost-Effectiveness: Addressing security early in the development process can be more cost-effective than attempting to patch vulnerabilities after a system is deployed.

- Compliance and Trust: Security by Design helps in meeting regulatory compliance requirements and builds trust with users and stakeholders by demonstrating a commitment to security.

Implementing Security by Design

- Security-Focused Culture: Cultivating a culture where security is a shared responsibility among all team members is crucial. This involves training and awareness programs to ensure that everyone understands the importance of security in the development process.

- Incorporating Security in Development Lifecycle: Security considerations should be embedded in every stage of the software development lifecycle (SDLC). From requirements gathering to design, coding, testing, and deployment, security should be an ongoing concern.

- Collaboration and Communication: Effective communication and collaboration among development, security, and operations teams are vital for implementing Security by Design. This ensures that security considerations are integrated seamlessly throughout the development process.

Implementing Security by Design can present challenges, including the need for additional resources, potential delays in development timelines, and the requirement for specialized security expertise. Overcoming these challenges requires a balanced approach that integrates security without compromising on functionality or user experience.

Personal Cybersecurity

In the digital age, personal devices like computers, smartphones, and tablets have become extensions of our identities, containing a vast array of personal and professional information. Securing these devices is essential to protect against various cyber threats, including data breaches, identity theft, and unauthorized access.

Personal devices are susceptible to a range of security threats. These include malware infections, phishing attacks, unauthorized access, data theft, and loss or theft of the device itself. The risks are compounded by the increasing sophistication of cyber attacks and the growing amount of sensitive data stored on these devices.

Securing Computers

Computers, whether desktops or laptops, are often the primary targets for cyber attacks due to the wealth of information they store and their frequent use in accessing sensitive online services.

- Use Reliable Antivirus Software: Installing and regularly updating reliable antivirus software can protect your computer from malware and other cyber threats.

- Regular Software Updates: Keeping the operating system and all software updated is crucial in safeguarding against vulnerabilities that can be exploited by attackers.

- Firewall Protection: Using a firewall helps to monitor and control incoming and outgoing network traffic based on predetermined security rules.

- Strong Passwords and Authentication: Implementing strong, unique passwords for all accounts and enabling two-factor authentication adds an extra layer of security.

- Backup Data Regularly: Regularly backing up important data ensures that it can be recovered in case of a cyber attack or hardware failure.

Securing Smartphones and Tablets

Smartphones and tablets are increasingly being targeted due to their portability and the vast amount of personal data they hold.

- Secure Lock Screens: Using a PIN, password, or biometric lock (like fingerprint or facial recognition) can prevent unauthorized access to your device.

- Update Operating Systems and Apps: Regular updates to your device's operating system and installed apps are vital in protecting against security vulnerabilities.

- Be Wary of App Permissions: Pay attention to the permissions requested by apps and avoid installing apps from untrusted sources.

- Use Secure Wi-Fi Connections: Be cautious when connecting to public Wi-Fi networks and consider using a VPN (Virtual Private Network) for secure browsing.

- Enable Remote Wiping and Location Tracking: In case of loss or theft, having the ability to remotely locate, lock, or wipe your device can protect your data from falling into the wrong hands.

General Best Practices for All Devices

- Be Vigilant Against Phishing and Scams: Educate yourself about the signs of phishing attempts and scams, which often target users through email, messages, or malicious websites.

- Use Encryption: Encrypting your device's hard drive adds an additional layer of security, making it difficult for attackers to access your data even if they gain physical access to your device.

- Secure Home Networks: Ensure your home Wi-Fi network is secure by using strong encryption (like WPA3), changing default usernames and passwords, and regularly updating your router's firmware.

- Be Cautious with Physical Security: Physical security is as important as digital. Be mindful of where you keep your devices, especially in public places, to avoid theft or loss.

Importance of Regular Software Updates

So, why are these updates so important and how do they contribute to overall cybersecurity?

Software updates, often released by software manufacturers, include a range of modifications. These updates may enhance the software's functionality, fix known bugs, patch security vulnerabilities, or improve the user interface. In the context of cybersecurity, updates are particularly critical as they often address security vulnerabilities that could be exploited by cybercriminals.

One of the primary purposes of regular software updates is to address security vulnerabilities. Developers continuously work to identify and fix vulnerabilities that could be exploited by attackers. Failing to install these updates leaves the door open for cybercriminals to exploit these weaknesses, potentially leading to data breaches, malware infections, and other cyber attacks.

Apart from security aspects, software updates often include improvements that enhance the performance of the software. This can include optimizing the software's speed, fixing bugs that may have been causing crashes or other problems, and introducing new features that improve user experience.

Regular software updates ensure that applications remain compatible with other software and operating systems. As technology evolves, new standards and protocols emerge, and keeping software updated is crucial for ensuring seamless interaction with other applications and services.

For businesses and organizations, staying up-to-date with software updates is often a part of regulatory compliance. Outdated software can lead to vulnerabilities that compromise customer data, potentially leading to legal and financial repercussions.

Managing Software Updates

- Automating Updates: One of the most effective strategies is to enable automatic updates where available. This ensures that software is updated as soon as a new version is released, without requiring manual intervention.

- Prioritizing Critical Updates: In environments where updates need to be controlled, such as in certain business settings, it's crucial to prioritize updates that address critical vulnerabilities.

- Employee Education and Policies: For organizations, educating employees about the importance of software updates and establishing clear policies for updating company devices is essential.

- Regular Audits and Monitoring: Conducting regular audits to ensure that all software used within an organization is up to date can help mitigate risks associated with outdated software.

While regular updating is crucial, it can present challenges. These include potential compatibility issues with existing systems, the need for downtime during updates, and the risk of updates introducing new bugs. Addressing these challenges requires a balanced approach, ensuring that updates are tested, especially in organizational settings, before wide-scale deployment.

Safe Browsing Practices

Online browsing, while convenient and efficient, exposes users to various risks, including malware infections, phishing scams, identity theft, and data breaches. These risks can emanate from malicious websites, insecure connections, and deceptive online content.

Basic safety rules:

- Recognizing and Avoiding Suspicious Websites: One of the first lines of defense in safe browsing is the ability to recognize and avoid suspicious websites. Malicious websites often mimic legitimate ones but may have odd URL structures, poor design, and spelling errors. These sites can infect your device with malware or trick you into disclosing sensitive information. Always verify the authenticity of a website, especially when it asks for personal or financial information.

- Using Secure Connections: Secure connections are vital in protecting the data you send and receive online. Always look for 'https' in the website's URL, which indicates that the site is using encryption to protect your data. Be cautious when using public Wi-Fi networks for sensitive transactions, as these networks are often unsecured and can be easily intercepted by cybercriminals.

- Implementing Strong Passwords and Authentication Methods: Using strong, unique passwords for different online accounts is crucial. This practice, combined with two-factor authentication (2FA), significantly enhances security. Two-factor authentication provides an additional layer of security beyond just the password, usually by requiring a code sent to your phone or email.

- Regularly Updating Browser and Security Software: Keeping your internet browser and security software updated is vital in protecting against the latest cyber threats. Developers regularly release updates that patch known security vulnerabilities. Ensure that your browser, antivirus, and other security tools are set to update automatically.

- Being Wary of Phishing Attempts: Phishing attacks, where cybercriminals disguise themselves as trustworthy entities to acquire sensitive information, are common online threats. Be cautious with emails, messages, or websites that ask for personal information, especially if they convey a sense of urgency or offer something that seems too good to be true.

- Managing Personal Information Online: Be mindful of the personal information you share online. Oversharing on social media platforms or other online forums can expose you to identity theft and other forms of cybercrime. Adjust privacy settings on social media to control who can see your information and posts.

- Using Ad Blockers and Anti-Tracking Tools: Ad blockers and anti-tracking tools can enhance your online privacy and security. These tools prevent intrusive ads that might contain malware and stop websites from tracking your online activities.

- Educating Yourself on Current Cyber Threats: Staying informed about current cyber threats can significantly improve your ability to browse safely. Awareness of the latest phishing tactics, malware trends, and online scams empowers you to recognize and avoid potential threats.

Managing Passwords

Passwords are a fundamental aspect of cybersecurity, serving as the first line of defense in protecting personal and organizational data. Passwords act as keys to our digital identities, granting access to personal accounts, sensitive information, and critical systems. They are the most common method of authentication used to verify a user's identity. The strength and management of these passwords play a significant role in safeguarding against unauthorized access and cyber attacks.

The strength of a password is determined by its complexity and unpredictability. Strong passwords are typically long, include a mix of upper and lower case letters, numbers, and special characters, and are unique to each account. They should not include easily guessable information like common words, phrases, or personal information. The rationale is that more complex passwords are harder for cybercriminals to crack using brute force or other hacking methods.

Many users fall into the trap of using simple, easily guessable passwords or reusing the same password across multiple accounts. This practice poses a significant security risk. If one account is compromised, all accounts sharing the same password become vulnerable. It's crucial to avoid common words, phrases, and personal information that can be easily guessed or obtained through social engineering.

Password Management Techniques

As the number of online accounts per individual rises, managing multiple strong, unique passwords becomes a challenge. This challenge can be addressed through:

- Password Managers: These tools store and manage your passwords in an encrypted database. They can generate strong passwords, store them securely, and autofill login information, making it easier to maintain unique passwords for each account.

- Two-Factor Authentication (2FA): Implementing 2FA adds an additional layer of security. Even if a password is compromised, the attacker would need a second factor – usually a code sent to a phone or email – to gain access.

- Regular Password Changes: Regularly updating passwords, especially for sensitive accounts, can help protect against ongoing threats. However, this practice should be balanced against the risk of creating weaker passwords due to frequent changes.

- Security Questions and Backup Authentication: Using security questions or backup authentication methods can provide alternate ways to access accounts if passwords are forgotten. However, it's important that answers to security questions are not easily guessable or publicly available information.

Educating Users about Password Security

Awareness and education are key components in effective password management. Users should be educated about the importance of strong passwords, the risks of password reuse, and how to use password management tools effectively.

Despite awareness, managing passwords remains a challenge for many. Users often struggle with remembering multiple complex passwords, leading to unsafe practices like writing them down or using simple, repeatable patterns. This challenge underscores the importance of user-friendly password management solutions.

As technology evolves, so do the approaches to authentication. Biometric authentication methods, like fingerprint and facial recognition, are becoming more common. There's also a growing trend towards password-less authentication methods, which use alternatives like one-time codes or physical tokens. These developments may change how we approach password security in the future.

Protecting Personal Data and Privacy Online

Personal data protection is not just about safeguarding one's identity, but it also encompasses the broader aspects of privacy, financial security, and personal safety. The information shared online can be exploited for identity theft, financial fraud, or even physical harm, making it imperative to be vigilant about how personal data is managed and shared online.

Secure Your Online Accounts: The first step in protecting personal data is to secure online accounts. This involves using strong, unique passwords for each account and enabling two-factor authentication where available. Be cautious about the personal information shared on social media platforms and adjust privacy settings to control who can view your information. Regularly reviewing and updating these settings is also important as social media platforms often change their privacy policies and settings.

Be Cautious with Public Wi-Fi: Public Wi-Fi networks, often found in places like coffee shops and airports, are convenient but can be insecure. Avoid conducting sensitive transactions, such as online banking or shopping, while connected to public Wi-Fi. If necessary, use a Virtual Private Network (VPN), which encrypts the internet connection and protects your data from being intercepted.

Understand and Manage Cookies: Cookies are small files stored on your computer by websites you visit, which are used to remember your preferences and track your online behavior. While they can enhance your browsing experience, they can also pose privacy concerns. Manage cookies in your browser settings, and consider using privacy-focused browsers or extensions that block third-party cookies.

Be Mindful of Phishing Scams: Phishing scams are a common tactic used by cybercriminals to trick individuals into revealing personal information. Be cautious of emails, messages, and websites that ask for personal data, especially if they convey urgency or appear suspicious. Verify the authenticity of requests for personal information and never click on links or download attachments from unknown or untrusted sources.

Regularly Update Software: Keeping software, including the operating system, antivirus programs, and apps, up to date is crucial. Software updates often include patches for security vulnerabilities that could be exploited to access your personal data.

Use Encrypted Communication: When sharing sensitive information, use encrypted communication methods. Services like encrypted email or messaging apps that offer end-to-end encryption ensure that only the intended recipient can read your messages.

Monitor Your Online Footprint: Regularly search for your name online to monitor your digital footprint. This can help you understand what information about you is publicly accessible and take steps to remove or secure it, if necessary.

Secure Your Home Network: Your home Wi-Fi network is a gateway to all your online activities. Secure it with a strong password, use the highest level of encryption available (like WPA3), and regularly update your router's firmware to protect against vulnerabilities.

Data Backups: Regularly back up important data to an external drive or a cloud-based service. In the event of a data breach or a cyber attack, you will have a backup of your critical data.

Educate Yourself and Others: Staying informed about the latest trends in cybersecurity and the common tactics used by cybercriminals is essential. Educate yourself and your family, especially children, about the importance of personal data protection and safe online habits.

Organizational Cybersecurity

Cybersecurity policies lay the foundation for a robust cybersecurity strategy, guiding the behavior of employees, the implementation of technologies, and the management of digital resources. Cybersecurity policies are essential for several reasons. They provide clear guidelines on how to handle and protect sensitive information, define roles and responsibilities related to cybersecurity, and ensure compliance with legal and regulatory requirements. A well-defined policy helps to minimize the risk of cyber attacks and data breaches, thereby protecting the organization's assets, reputation, and trustworthiness.

Key Components of Cybersecurity Policies

1. Scope and Objectives: The policy should clearly define its scope, covering all aspects of the organization's information technology environment. The objectives of the policy should align with the organization's overall security strategy.

2. Roles and Responsibilities: Clearly defined roles and responsibilities ensure that every member of the organization understands their part in maintaining cybersecurity.

3. Data Classification and Protection: Guidelines on classifying data according to its sensitivity and the corresponding protection measures required for each classification level.

4. Access Control: Rules and procedures for granting, modifying, and revoking access to systems and data, including the use of strong authentication methods.

5. Incident Response and Reporting: Procedures for managing and reporting cybersecurity incidents to ensure timely and effective responses.

6. User Behavior and Security Awareness: Guidelines on acceptable use of the organization's IT resources, and policies to promote security awareness among employees.

7. Regular Audits and Compliance Checks: Procedures for conducting regular audits of cybersecurity practices and ensuring compliance with relevant laws and regulations.

Implementing Cybersecurity Policies

The development of cybersecurity policies should involve stakeholders from various departments, including IT, human resources, legal, and executive leadership. This ensures that the policy is comprehensive and aligns with all aspects of the organization.

- Risk Assessment: A thorough risk assessment should inform the development of cybersecurity policies, identifying potential threats and vulnerabilities.

- Customization to the Organization: Cybersecurity policies should be tailored to the specific needs and characteristics of the organization, considering factors like size, industry, and the nature of the data handled.

- Clear and Concise Language: Policies should be written in clear, concise language to ensure they are easily understood by all employees.

- Training and Awareness: Employees should be trained on the cybersecurity policies and their importance. Regular refreshers and updates on new threats and policies are crucial.

Maintaining and Updating Policies

Cybersecurity policies are not static documents; they require regular review and updates to remain effective. Changes in technology, emerging threats, and new business processes can all necessitate updates to policies.

- Regular Reviews: Schedule regular reviews of cybersecurity policies to ensure they remain relevant and effective.

- Feedback Mechanisms: Implement mechanisms to gather feedback on the effectiveness of policies and to identify areas for improvement.

- Change Management: Establish a process for managing changes to policies, ensuring that updates are communicated effectively and implemented efficiently.

Implementing cybersecurity policies can present challenges, including resistance from employees, the complexity of monitoring compliance, and the need to balance security with usability. Overcoming these challenges requires a commitment to a security-conscious culture, ongoing training, and engagement with employees.

Employee Training and Awareness Programs

In the realm of cybersecurity, the human element is often considered the weakest link. Employees can either be a first line of defense or a significant vulnerability, depending on their awareness and understanding of cybersecurity practices. Employee training and awareness programs are critical in equipping staff with the knowledge and skills needed to protect themselves and the organization from cyber threats.

The rapidly evolving nature of cyber threats makes regular employee training not just beneficial but necessary. With the majority of security breaches involving some form of human error, such as falling for phishing scams or mishandling data, informed and vigilant staff are a crucial component of an organization's overall cybersecurity posture.

Core Components of Training and Awareness Programs

- Understanding Cyber Threats: Employees should be educated about the types of cyber threats, such as phishing, malware, ransomware, and social engineering attacks, and the potential consequences of these threats to the organization.

- Best Practices for Digital Security: Training programs should cover the best practices for digital security, including strong password creation, safe internet browsing, secure handling of sensitive data, and adherence to the organization's cybersecurity policies.

- Recognizing and Reporting Incidents: Employees need to be able to recognize the signs of a cyber incident and understand the procedures for reporting these incidents. Prompt reporting can significantly reduce the impact of a cyber attack.

- Regular Updates and Refresher Courses: Given the dynamic nature of cyber threats, regular updates and refresher courses are essential to keep employees informed about the latest threats and protective measures.

Tailoring Training to Different Roles

Not all employees face the same level of risk, and as such, cybersecurity training should be tailored to the specific needs and risks associated with different roles within the organization. For instance, staff with access to sensitive data may require more in-depth training compared to those with limited access.

The effectiveness of training programs is often contingent on their ability to engage participants. Interactive training methods, such as simulations, workshops, and gamification, can be more effective in imparting knowledge and skills than traditional lecture-based approaches.

Beyond formal training programs, fostering a culture of security within the organization is crucial. This involves creating an environment where cybersecurity is a shared responsibility and encouraging behaviors that promote security, such as questioning unusual requests and reporting potential threats.

To ensure the effectiveness of training and awareness programs, organizations should measure their impact. This can be done through assessments, feedback surveys, and monitoring the incidence of security-related incidents. Adjustments to the training program should be made based on these evaluations.

Implementing effective training and awareness programs can present challenges, including limited resources, employee disengagement, and the difficulty of keeping content up to date. Addressing these challenges requires an innovative training approaches, and the allocation of sufficient resources.

Securing Organizational Networks

In the digital landscape, organizational networks are constantly under threat from various cyber attacks. These networks, being the backbone of IT infrastructure in most organizations, require robust security measures to protect sensitive data and ensure uninterrupted business operations.

Organizational networks are intricate systems often encompassing a wide range of devices, applications, and data. They are targeted for the valuable information they hold and their integral role in business operations. A breach in network security can lead to significant data loss, financial damages, and reputational harm. Therefore, securing these networks is paramount.

Basic safety practices:

Comprehensive Risk Assessment: A thorough risk assessment is the first step in securing organizational networks. This involves identifying potential vulnerabilities in the network, the various threats that could exploit these vulnerabilities, and the potential impact of such exploits. Understanding the risk landscape helps in prioritizing security measures and allocating resources effectively.

Network Segmentation and Access Control

- Network Segmentation: Dividing the network into smaller, manageable segments can significantly enhance security. If one segment is compromised, the breach can be contained, preventing it from spreading across the entire network.

- Access Control: Implementing strict access control policies ensures that only authorized personnel have access to sensitive parts of the network. This includes managing user privileges based on roles and responsibilities and ensuring proper authentication mechanisms are in place.

Firewalls and Intrusion Prevention Systems: Firewalls act as a barrier between trusted internal networks and untrusted external networks. Configuring firewalls to filter out unauthorized access and potentially malicious traffic is crucial. Intrusion Prevention Systems (IPS) complement firewalls by identifying and blocking known threats.

Regular Software Updates and Patch Management: Keeping all network software up to date, including operating systems, applications, and security tools, is essential in protecting against known vulnerabilities. A robust patch management process ensures that these updates are implemented promptly and efficiently.

Monitoring and Incident Response: Continuous monitoring of network activity allows for the early detection of unusual patterns that may indicate a security breach. Having an incident response plan in place ensures that any breach is addressed quickly and effectively, minimizing damage.

Secure Wireless Networks: Wireless networks are particularly vulnerable to security breaches. Securing these networks involves using strong encryption protocols, hiding the network SSID, and ensuring firmware is regularly updated.

Employee Training and Awareness: Employees are often the first line of defense against network attacks. Regular training and awareness programs on network security best practices, such as identifying phishing attempts and safe internet browsing, are critical.

Use of Encryption: Encrypting data transmitted across the network protects it from interception and unauthorized access. This is particularly important for sensitive information and communications.

Regular Security Audits: Conducting regular security audits helps in identifying and addressing vulnerabilities in the network. These audits should be comprehensive, covering hardware, software, and policies.

Implementation of VPNs: Virtual Private Networks (VPNs) provide secure access to the organizational network, particularly for remote workers. They encrypt data transmitted over the internet, protecting it from interception.

Securing organizational networks is a complex task, challenged by the evolving nature of cyber threats, the integration of new technologies, and the need to balance security with usability.

Data Protection and Backup Strategies

Effective data protection and backup strategies are essential in safeguarding against data loss due to various threats, including cyber attacks, natural disasters, and human error.

Data protection and backup are critical components of an organization's overall cybersecurity and risk management strategy. They ensure the integrity, availability, and confidentiality of data, which is crucial for maintaining business continuity, complying with legal and regulatory requirements, and protecting the organization's reputation.

A comprehensive data protection strategy involves a range of measures designed to safeguard data from unauthorized access, corruption, and loss. This includes implementing strong access controls, encrypting sensitive data, and regularly updating security software. It also involves ensuring compliance with data protection regulations and standards relevant to the organization's industry and location.

Implementing Effective Backup Solutions

Effective backup solutions are the cornerstone of any data protection strategy. These solutions ensure that critical data can be recovered and restored in the event of loss or damage.

1. Regular Backups: Regularly backing up data is crucial. The frequency of backups should be based on the criticality of the data and the rate at which it changes.

2. Diverse Backup Methods: Employing diverse backup methods, such as on-site backups for quick access and off-site or cloud backups for disaster recovery, provides a comprehensive approach to data protection.

3. Testing Backup Systems: Regular testing of backup systems is essential to ensure they function correctly when needed. This includes testing the restoration process to verify that data can be effectively recovered.

The 3-2-1 Backup Rule: A widely recommended approach for backup is the 3-2-1 rule: keep three copies of your data (one primary and two backups), store the backups on two different types of media, and keep one backup copy offsite.

This rule provides a solid framework for protecting data against a variety of loss scenarios.

Ensuring Data Redundancy: Data redundancy, where duplicate copies of data are stored in different physical locations, is crucial in protecting against data loss due to natural disasters, fires, or other catastrophic events. Cloud storage solutions often provide built-in redundancy across multiple geographic locations.

Disaster Recovery Planning: An effective data protection and backup strategy includes a comprehensive disaster recovery plan. This plan outlines the procedures for recovering data and restoring operations in the event of a disaster. It should include defined roles and responsibilities, detailed recovery procedures, and a communication plan for stakeholders.

Addressing the Challenges in Data Protection and Backup: Implementing data protection and backup strategies can present challenges, including managing the costs of storage and backup solutions, ensuring the security of backup data, and addressing the complexities of backing up diverse data types and systems. Overcoming these challenges requires careful planning, regular review and adjustment of strategies, and investment in reliable backup and storage technologies.

Encryption in Data Protection: Encrypting backup data adds an additional layer of security, protecting the data from unauthorized access if the backup media or storage is compromised. Encryption should be implemented both in transit and at rest.

Maintaining Compliance and Data Sovereignty: Organizations must ensure that their data protection and backup strategies comply with relevant data protection laws and regulations. This includes considerations around data sovereignty, which refers to the legal implications of storing data in different geographic locations.

Incident Response and Disaster Recovery Planning

Incident response and disaster recovery planning are critical components of a comprehensive cybersecurity strategy. It refers to the methodology an organization uses to respond to and manage a cyberattack or data breach. A well-structured incident response plan aims to minimize damage, reduce recovery time and costs, and mitigate the exploited vulnerabilities.

Developing an Incident Response Plan

The development of an incident response plan involves several key steps:

1. Preparation: This involves setting up an incident response team, defining roles and responsibilities, and equipping them with the necessary tools and resources.

2. Identification: The ability to quickly identify an incident is crucial. This involves monitoring systems and networks for signs of security breaches and having processes in place to detect and report incidents.

3. Containment: Once an incident is identified, containing it is critical to prevent further damage. This may involve isolating affected systems or networks.

4. Eradication and Recovery: After containment, the focus shifts to eradicating the threat and recovering affected systems to normal operation. This includes repairing and patching systems, and restoring data from backups.

5. Post-Incident Analysis: After an incident, analyzing what happened, how it was handled, and what can be improved is vital for strengthening future responses.

Disaster recovery planning is broader than incident response, encompassing not just cyberattacks but any event that could disrupt business operations, such as natural disasters or power outages. It focuses on restoring IT operations and minimizing business interruptions.

Key Elements of Disaster Recovery Planning

Risk Assessment and Business Impact Analysis: Assessing the risks to business operations and conducting a business impact analysis helps in understanding which systems and processes are critical and the potential impact of their disruption.

Disaster Recovery Strategies: This involves developing strategies to recover IT systems, applications, and data that are critical for business operations. This includes identifying which systems need to be recovered first (based on their criticality) and setting recovery time objectives.

Data Backup Solutions: A robust data backup solution is a cornerstone of disaster recovery. This involves regular backups and storing backup data in a secure and preferably offsite location.

Communication Plan: Having a clear communication plan is crucial during a disaster. This involves communication within the organization and with external stakeholders, including customers and partners.

Testing and Maintenance: Regular testing of the disaster recovery plan ensures its effectiveness. The plan should be updated regularly to reflect changes in the business environment and IT infrastructure.

Challenges

Implementing effective incident response and disaster recovery plans can be challenging. It requires a coordinated effort across the organization, investment in the right tools and technologies, and continuous training and awareness programs for employees. Keeping the plans updated and tested in a rapidly changing technology landscape is also a significant challenge.

Effective incident response and disaster recovery require strong leadership and governance. Senior management should be involved in developing and supporting these plans, ensuring that they align with the organization's overall risk management and business continuity strategies.

Cybersecurity Technologies

Firewalls and Intrusion Detection Systems

In the field of cybersecurity, firewalls and intrusion detection systems (IDS) are essential components of an organization's defense strategy. They serve as critical tools in safeguarding network security by controlling incoming and outgoing network traffic and identifying potential threats.

Firewalls act as a barrier between a trusted internal network and untrusted external networks, such as the internet. A firewall typically works by filtering incoming and outgoing traffic based on an established set of security rules. These rules determine which traffic is allowed to enter or leave the network, thus protecting the internal network from unauthorized access and various types of cyber attacks.

Types of Firewalls

- Packet-Filtering Firewalls: These are the most basic type of firewalls that control network access by monitoring outgoing and incoming packets and either allowing them to pass or halting them based on the source and destination Internet Protocol (IP) addresses, protocols, and ports.

- Stateful Inspection Firewalls: These firewalls keep track of the state of active connections and make decisions based on the context of the traffic and state of the connection, which offers more security than simple packet filtering.

- Proxy Firewalls: Acting as an intermediary between users and the services they access, proxy firewalls evaluate requests at the application layer and can prevent direct connections between networks, which adds a layer of security.

- Next-Generation Firewalls (NGFW): These offer a more sophisticated solution by combining traditional firewall technology with additional functionalities like encrypted traffic inspection, intrusion prevention systems, and identity-based and application-aware functionalities.

Intrusion Detection Systems

Intrusion Detection Systems are designed to detect and alert organizations to potential threats, such as breaches, malware infections, and other malicious activities. They monitor network traffic for suspicious activity and generate alerts when such activity is detected. IDS play a crucial role in identifying cyber threats that might bypass firewalls.

Types of Intrusion Detection Systems

- Network-Based IDS (NIDS): These systems monitor network traffic for suspicious activity and alert administrators about potential threats. They are placed at strategic points within the network to monitor traffic to and from all devices on the network.

- Host-Based IDS (HIDS): HIDS are installed on individual devices (or hosts) and monitor inbound and outbound traffic from the device, as well as system configurations and application activity.

- Signature-Based Detection: This method involves searching for specific patterns, such as byte sequences in network traffic, or known malicious instruction sequences used by malware.

- Anomaly-Based Detection: Anomaly-based IDS detect unusual patterns or behaviors, such as a high amount of traffic at an unusual time of day, which could signify a cyber attack.

Integration of Firewalls and IDS

Integrating firewalls and IDS creates a more robust security system. While the firewall controls access to the network by filtering incoming and outgoing traffic based on predefined rules, the IDS monitors and analyzes the traffic that passes through the firewall to identify potential threats. This layered security approach ensures better protection against a wide range of cyber threats.

Implementing firewalls and IDS involves certain challenges, including managing false positives in intrusion detection, keeping up with evolving cyber threats, and integrating these systems within existing IT infrastructure. Best practices include regular updates and patches to firewall and IDS software, fine-tuning IDS to minimize false positives and false negatives, and continuous monitoring and analysis of firewall logs and IDS alerts.

Antivirus and Anti-malware Software

Antivirus and anti-malware software are essential tools in the fight against malicious software, such as viruses, worms, trojans, ransomware, and spyware. While the term 'antivirus' traditionally referred to software designed specifically to detect and remove computer viruses, the term has evolved. Today, antivirus software typically encompasses a broader range of capabilities, often covering multiple types of malware.

How Antivirus and Anti-malware Software Work

These software programs typically work by scanning files and directories for patterns of malicious behavior or known malware signatures. This involves comparing the content of a file to a database of known malware signatures - unique strings of data or characteristics of known malicious software. In addition to signature-based detection, modern antivirus programs often employ heuristic and behavior-based detection methods to identify new, previously unknown malware.

- Heuristic-based Detection: This method involves examining the behavior of programs to detect unknown or new malware types that have not yet been added to signature databases.

- Behavior-based Detection: This technique monitors the behavior of programs and flags suspicious activities that could indicate malicious actions, even if the specific malware is not in the signature database.

The effectiveness of antivirus and anti-malware software heavily depends on the currency of their malware databases. As new malware variants are continuously developed and released into the digital world, it's crucial that these software programs are regularly updated to ensure they can recognize and protect against the latest threats.

Despite advances in antivirus and anti-malware technology, detecting malware remains a challenge. Cybercriminals continually develop sophisticated methods to evade detection, including polymorphic and metamorphic malware, and fileless malware that operates in computer memory without writing files to the disk.

While antivirus and anti-malware software are critical, they should not be the sole line of defense. They are most effective when used in conjunction with other cybersecurity measures, such as firewalls, intrusion detection systems, and safe browsing practices.

Best Practices for Using Antivirus and Anti-malware Software

- Comprehensive Protection Strategy: Utilize antivirus and anti-malware software as part of a broader, layered cybersecurity strategy.

- Regular Updates and Scans: Ensure that the software is set to update automatically and perform regular scans.

- Educating Users: Educate users about safe computing practices to prevent malware infections, as human error is a common cause of malware infections.

- Backup and Recovery: Maintain regular backups of critical data as a safeguard against data loss due to malware infections.

Selecting the right antivirus and anti-malware software involves considering factors such as the level of protection needed, ease of use, system compatibility, and the balance between protection and system performance. It's advisable to choose reputable solutions that are regularly updated and provide comprehensive protection against a wide range of threats.

Virtual Private Networks (VPNs)

When data security and privacy are paramount, Virtual Private Networks (VPNs) have become an essential tool for individuals and organizations alike. VPNs provide an additional layer of security and privacy for internet connections, especially in environments where network security cannot be assured.

A Virtual Private Network, or VPN, is a service that creates a secure, encrypted connection over a less secure network, such as the public internet. The primary purpose of a VPN is to provide privacy and security to data traffic by routing it through a VPN server, where it is encrypted. This setup shields the user's online activities and personal information from external threats, including hackers, governments, and internet service providers.

How VPNs Enhance Security and Privacy

- Data Encryption: VPNs encrypt data transmitted over the internet, making it difficult for unauthorized parties to intercept and decipher it. This encryption is crucial for protecting sensitive information, particularly when using public Wi-Fi networks.

- IP Address Masking: By routing traffic through a VPN server, the user's IP address is masked, making it difficult to track the user's location and browsing activities.

- Secure Access to Networks: VPNs are often used by organizations to provide employees with secure access to internal networks, especially when working remotely.

When a user connects to a VPN service, their data traffic is sent through an encrypted tunnel to a VPN server, which then connects to the desired online destination, such as a website. This process not only encrypts the data but also masks the user's IP address. The VPN server, in this case, acts as a sort of middleman, preventing the user's internet service provider (ISP) or any other third party from viewing the data or determining its origin.

Types of VPNs

- Remote Access VPNs: These are used by individuals to secure their internet connection. They allow users to access the internet through a private network, even when they are using a public network.

- Site-to-Site VPNs: Commonly used by organizations, these VPNs connect the networks of different offices or locations, creating a single, unified network.

Choosing the Right VPN Service

When selecting a VPN service, several factors need to be considered:

- Security Protocols: Look for VPNs that offer robust security protocols, such as OpenVPN or L2TP/IPsec, which provide strong encryption.

- Server Locations: The availability of multiple server locations can be beneficial for speed and accessing geo-restricted content.

- Privacy Policies: Ensure the VPN provider has a strict no-logs policy, meaning they do not track or store information about your online activities.

- Speed and Reliability: A good VPN should provide a stable connection without significantly slowing down internet speed.

For organizations, VPNs are crucial for enabling secure remote access to corporate networks and protecting data communication. They play a key role in implementing flexible work arrangements, such as work-from-home policies, by ensuring that employees can access internal resources securely from remote locations.

Potential Limitations

While VPNs provide enhanced security and privacy, they are not infallible. The VPN provider itself could potentially access your data, making the choice of provider critical. Additionally, VPNs may not protect against all forms of tracking, such as cookies placed on websites. Users should remain aware of other cybersecurity best practices, even when using a VPN.

Biometric Security Systems

Biometric security systems, which use unique physical or behavioral characteristics to identify individuals, have become increasingly prevalent in both personal and organizational security frameworks. As technology advances, biometric systems offer a sophisticated and often more secure alternative to traditional forms of security such as passwords and PINs.

Commonly used biometric identifiers include fingerprints, facial recognition, iris scans, voice recognition, and hand geometry. These systems work by comparing a person's biometric data with stored, pre-recorded data. If the two sets of data match, the individual is granted access.

Applications of Biometric Security

Biometric systems have a wide range of applications across various sectors:

- Personal Devices: Smartphones and laptops increasingly use fingerprints and facial recognition for unlocking devices and authenticating payments.

- Access Control in Organizations: Biometric systems are used to control access to physical locations like offices, data centers, and restricted areas within businesses.

- Time and Attendance Monitoring: In workplaces, biometrics like fingerprint scanning are used for timekeeping and managing employee attendance.

- Law Enforcement and Public Security: Governments and law enforcement agencies use biometrics for identification purposes, including in passports, ID cards, and databases used for security screening.

Advantages of Biometric Security

- Increased Security: Biometrics offer a high level of security as they are difficult to replicate or steal compared to traditional passwords or ID cards.

- Convenience: Biometrics provide a convenient method of authentication, often faster and easier than remembering passwords or carrying identification cards.

- Non-Transferability: Since biometric attributes are inherently linked to an individual, they eliminate the risk associated with transferable authentication methods like ID cards or access tokens.

Challenges and Considerations in Biometric Systems

- Privacy Concerns: The use of biometric data raises significant privacy concerns. There's a risk of misuse of sensitive biometric data if it is not stored or managed properly.

- Security of Biometric Data: While biometric data is unique, it's not infallible. Biometric systems can be susceptible to spoofing, and once compromised, biometric data cannot be changed like a password.

- Integration and Cost: Integrating biometric systems into existing security frameworks can be complex and expensive, especially for large organizations.

- False Rejections and Acceptances: Like any security system, biometrics is not perfect and can result in false rejections (denying access to authorized persons) or false acceptances (allowing access to unauthorized persons).

The use of biometric data entails navigating ethical and legal considerations. Issues such as informed consent for the collection of biometric data, the potential for discriminatory practices, and compliance with data protection laws are critical factors to consider.

Emerging trends include the development of more sophisticated and accurate biometric systems, such as heart rate or gait recognition, and the integration of biometrics with artificial intelligence to enhance security and user experience.

Cybersecurity Best Practices

Regular security audits are a critical aspect of maintaining and enhancing an organization's cybersecurity posture. These audits involve a systematic evaluation of the security of an organization's information system by measuring how well it conforms to a set of established criteria.

The primary goal of regular security audits is to identify vulnerabilities and risks in an organization's IT infrastructure. In the dynamic landscape of cyber threats, where new vulnerabilities and attack vectors continually emerge, regular audits help ensure that security measures are not only effective but also adaptive to new challenges.

The Process of Conducting Security Audits

A comprehensive security audit typically involves several key steps:

- Planning: This initial phase involves defining the scope of the audit, identifying the systems and processes to be examined, and determining the criteria against which these will be evaluated.

- Data Collection: The auditor gathers relevant information about the organization's IT infrastructure, security policies, and control mechanisms. This may include reviewing documentations, system configurations, and security settings.

- Risk Assessment: Analyzing the collected data to identify vulnerabilities and assess the potential risks associated with these vulnerabilities. This assessment considers the likelihood of a security breach and its potential impact on the organization.

- Evaluation and Reporting: Comparing the organization's security practices against the established criteria to determine their effectiveness. The findings, including any security gaps and non-compliance issues, are documented in a detailed report.

- Recommendations and Action Plan: Providing recommendations for addressing identified vulnerabilities and risks, and assisting in developing an action plan for implementing these recommendations.

Types of Security Audits

- Internal Audits: Conducted by the organization's own audit team, internal audits are a self-check mechanism to ensure compliance with internal security policies and standards.

- External Audits: Performed by independent third-party auditors, external audits provide an unbiased assessment of the organization's cybersecurity posture.

- Regulatory Compliance Audits: These are specialized audits conducted to ensure compliance with specific regulatory requirements, such as GDPR, HIPAA, or PCI-DSS.

Benefits

- Enhanced Security: Regular audits help in identifying and addressing vulnerabilities, thereby enhancing the overall security of the organization.

- Compliance Assurance: Audits ensure that the organization complies with relevant laws, regulations, and industry standards, reducing the risk of legal penalties and fines.

- Improved Risk Management: By identifying potential risks, audits enable organizations to develop more effective risk management strategies.

- Increased Stakeholder Confidence: Regular audits demonstrate a commitment to cybersecurity, enhancing the trust of customers, partners, and stakeholders.

Conducting thorough and effective security audits can present challenges, including the allocation of sufficient resources, dealing with complex IT environments, and keeping up with the evolving nature of cyber threats. These challenges require a structured approach, skilled personnel, and sometimes the engagement of external experts.

Best Practices for Security Audits

- Regular Schedule: Establishing a regular schedule for audits ensures that security assessments are not overlooked and that security measures remain up-to-date.

- Comprehensive Scope: Audits should cover all aspects of the organization's cybersecurity, including physical security, network security, and employee training programs.

- Continuous Improvement: The findings from audits should be used as a basis for continuous improvement in the organization's cybersecurity practices.

- Stakeholder Involvement: Engaging various stakeholders, including IT staff, management, and end-users, in the audit process can provide valuable insights and foster a culture of security awareness.

The Principle of Least Privilege

The Principle of Least Privilege (PoLP) is a fundamental concept in the field of computer security, advocating for the minimal user profile permissions necessary to perform its functions. The application of this principle is essential in creating a secure computing environment.

At its core, the Principle of Least Privilege requires that all users, applications, and systems operate using the least amount of privilege necessary. This means that access rights are granted only to the extent required to perform authorized tasks. For instance, a regular employee of a company should not have access to sensitive financial records if their job function does not require it. Similarly, an application running on a computer system should have only the permissions necessary for its operation and no more.

Implementing the Principle of Least Privilege can be challenging, especially in complex organizations with multiple users and roles. It involves an initial assessment of the access requirements of all users, software, and systems. This assessment must be thorough and continuously updated to reflect changes within the organization, such as changes in job roles or the introduction of new technologies.

- User Access Management: This involves assigning permissions based on job roles and responsibilities. Access rights should be regularly reviewed and adjusted as job roles change or evolve.

- Application Permissions: Applications should be granted only the permissions necessary for their function. This reduces the risk of malicious software exploiting excess privileges to cause harm.

- System Access Controls: System-level access should be tightly controlled and monitored. Administrative privileges should be restricted to a minimum number of users.

Benefits

- Reduced Attack Surface: By limiting the number of users with access to critical systems and data, the principle reduces the chances of a successful attack.

- Minimized Impact of Breaches: In the event of a breach, the principle ensures that the damage is contained to a limited area, thereby reducing its overall impact.

- Enhanced Compliance: Many regulatory frameworks emphasize the importance of access control in maintaining data security. Implementing the Principle of Least Privilege helps in meeting these regulatory requirements.

Challenges and Considerations

While the benefits of implementing the Principle of Least Privilege are clear, it does come with challenges:

- Balancing Security and Usability: Overly restrictive access controls can hinder productivity and user experience. Finding the right balance between security and usability is key.

- Complexity in Large Organizations: In large organizations with multiple roles and systems, implementing and managing least privilege access can be complex and resource-intensive.

- Continuous Management and Monitoring: The Principle of Least Privilege requires ongoing management and monitoring to remain effective. This involves regular audits and adjustments to access rights.

Best Practices

- Role-Based Access Control (RBAC): Implementing RBAC helps in efficiently managing user permissions based on their role within the organization.

- Regular Audits and Reviews: Conducting regular audits of access rights ensures that privileges remain aligned with job requirements.

- Employing Automation Tools: Using automation tools for managing access rights can reduce the complexity and resource requirements of implementing the principle.

Patch Management

Patch management is the process of managing updates (patches) for software and systems. These patches are often released by vendors to address security vulnerabilities, fix bugs, or improve functionality. Effective patch management ensures that these updates are systematically tested, approved, and applied to ensure the ongoing security and stability of IT environments. As software vulnerabilities are constantly identified and exploited by cybercriminals, the importance of an effective patch management strategy cannot be overstated.

The primary purpose of patch management is to protect systems against known vulnerabilities. Cybercriminals frequently exploit these vulnerabilities to gain unauthorized access, disrupt services, or steal sensitive data. By keeping software and systems up to date, organizations can mitigate these risks. Additionally, patch management contributes to the overall performance and efficiency of IT systems.

The Patch Management Process

- Inventory Management: The first step in patch management is having a clear inventory of all the software and systems within the organization. This inventory helps in understanding what needs to be patched and prioritizing updates based on criticality.

- Patch Testing: Before applying a patch to a live environment, it is essential to test it in a controlled setting. This testing ensures that the patch does not adversely affect system functionality or compatibility.

- Approval and Deployment: Once a patch has been tested, it should be formally approved for deployment. The deployment process should be carefully planned to minimize disruption to business operations.

- Monitoring and Reporting: After deployment, ongoing monitoring is necessary to ensure that patches have been applied successfully and to identify any issues that may arise. Regular reporting helps in maintaining visibility over the patch management process.

Challenges in Patch Management

- Resource Constraints: Patch management can be resource-intensive, requiring dedicated personnel and time for testing and deployment.

- Complex IT Environments: In organizations with complex IT environments, coordinating patches across various systems and software can be challenging.

- Keeping Up with Vulnerabilities: The rapid emergence of new vulnerabilities requires a proactive approach to patch management. Organizations must stay informed about the latest security threats and corresponding patches.

- Balancing Security and Business Needs: Timing patch deployments to minimize impact on business operations requires careful planning and coordination.

Best Practices in Patch Management

- Automated Patch Management Tools: Utilizing automated tools can streamline the patch management process, ensuring timely and consistent application of patches.

- Prioritization of Patches: Prioritize patches based on the criticality of the vulnerabilities they address and the importance of the affected systems to business operations.

- Regular Audits and Compliance: Regular audits of patch management practices help ensure compliance with internal policies and external regulations.

- Stakeholder Communication: Keeping relevant stakeholders informed about planned updates, potential impacts, and any required actions is essential for a smooth patch management process.

- Continuous Improvement: Continuously evaluate and improve the patch management process based on lessons learned from previous deployments and changes in the IT environment.

Multi-Factor Authentication

In the domain of cybersecurity, Multi-Factor Authentication (MFA) has emerged as a critical defense mechanism against the increasing incidents of data breaches and identity thefts. MFA enhances security by requiring users to provide two or more verification factors to gain access to a resource such as an application, online account, or a VPN.

Multi-Factor Authentication involves combining two or more independent credentials: what the user knows (password), what the user has (security token), and what the user is (biometric verification). The idea is that even if one factor is compromised, unauthorized access to the user's account is still not possible without at least one additional verification method.

The traditional single-factor authentication, like a password or PIN, has proven insufficient against modern cyber threats. Passwords can be easily compromised through phishing, social engineering, or brute force attacks. MFA adds layers of security, making it significantly more challenging for unauthorized persons to breach accounts or access sensitive information.

Types of Authentication Factors

- Knowledge Factors: Something the user knows, such as a password, PIN, or answers to security questions.

- Possession Factors: Something the user has, like a security token, a smartphone app, or a smart card.

- Inherence Factors: Something that is inherent to the user, typically a biometric characteristic like fingerprints, facial recognition, or voice recognition.

Implementing Multi-Factor Authentication

Implementing MFA requires careful planning and consideration of user experience and security needs. It involves selecting appropriate factors that provide robust security without overly complicating the authentication process.

- User Education and Training: Users must be educated about the importance of MFA and trained on how to use it. Understanding the role of MFA in protecting their information can encourage user acceptance and compliance.

- Balancing Security and Convenience: While MFA significantly enhances security, it can also add complexity to the authentication process. Organizations need to balance the level of security with the need for user convenience to avoid reducing productivity or user satisfaction.

- Choosing the Right MFA Tools: There are various MFA tools and solutions available. Organizations should choose solutions that align with their specific security requirements and are compatible with their existing IT infrastructure.

Challenges in Multi-Factor Authentication

Despite its benefits, MFA can present challenges, including potential resistance from users due to added steps in the authentication process, the need for additional resources to manage the MFA system, and potential technical issues with authentication factors, like lost tokens or phones.

- To effectively implement MFA and overcome these challenges, organizations should:

- Provide Clear Communication: Clearly communicating the need and benefits of MFA to users can help in mitigating resistance.

- Offer User Support: Providing timely support for users encountering issues with MFA can reduce frustration and downtime.

- Regularly Review and Update MFA Practices: MFA systems and practices should be regularly reviewed and updated to address emerging threats and changing user needs.

The future of MFA is likely to see more sophisticated methods of authentication, including advancements in biometrics and behavioral analytics. As technology evolves, so will the methods of authentication, making them more secure, user-friendly, and integrated into users' daily routines.

Continuous Monitoring and Reporting

In an environment where cyber threats are continually evolving and becoming more sophisticated, continuous monitoring and reporting are indispensable for maintaining robust security. Continuous monitoring in cybersecurity is the practice of constantly scanning and assessing the security posture of an organization's IT environment. This includes keeping track of network traffic, user activities, system logs, and vulnerabilities. The primary objective is to detect and respond to threats as quickly as possible, thus minimizing their potential impact.

Key Components of Continuous Monitoring

- Real-time Data Collection: This involves gathering data from various sources within the IT infrastructure, including network devices, servers, and applications. The data collected provides insight into ongoing activities and potential security incidents.

- Automated Analysis and Alerting: The data collected is analyzed in real-time using automated tools. These tools are designed to identify patterns or activities that indicate a potential security threat. When a threat is detected, the system generates alerts to notify relevant personnel.

- Integration of Security Tools: Continuous monitoring often involves the integration of various security tools, such as intrusion detection systems, firewalls, and antivirus software. This integration allows for a more comprehensive view of the security landscape.

Reporting is a critical aspect of continuous monitoring. It involves the documentation and communication of security findings to stakeholders within the organization. This includes generating regular reports on the overall security status, incidents detected, and actions taken.

Benefits

- Early Detection of Threats: Continuous monitoring allows for the early detection of security threats, enabling organizations to respond swiftly and mitigate potential damage.

- Compliance with Regulations: Many industries have regulatory requirements for continuous monitoring and reporting of security systems. Regular compliance reports can be generated to demonstrate adherence to these regulations.

- Enhanced Security Posture: Continuous monitoring provides a dynamic view of an organization's security posture, allowing for quick adjustments and improvements in response to emerging threats.

- Informed Decision Making: Regular reporting provides valuable insights into security trends and vulnerabilities, aiding in informed decision-making regarding security strategies and investments.

Challenges

Implementing a continuous monitoring and reporting system can present several challenges:

- Resource Intensiveness: Continuous monitoring requires significant resources, including specialized tools and skilled personnel to manage and analyze the data.

- Data Overload: The vast amount of data generated can be overwhelming, making it difficult to identify genuine threats among false positives.

- Maintaining Accuracy: Ensuring the accuracy and relevance of monitoring tools and methods is crucial, as outdated tools or improper configurations can lead to missed threats.

Best Practices for Effective Continuous Monitoring

- Tailored Monitoring Strategies: Develop monitoring strategies that are tailored to the specific needs and risks of the organization.

- Skilled Personnel: Employ or train skilled cybersecurity personnel to manage and analyze monitoring data effectively.

- Balancing Automation with Human Oversight: While automation is key in handling the volume of data, human oversight is essential for interpreting complex threats and reducing false positives.

Dealing with Cyber Incidents

Cyber incidents, which range from data breaches to network intrusions, can have significant implications for business operations, data security, and organizational reputation. Identifying cyber incidents promptly is essential for minimizing their impact. This process involves monitoring various systems and networks for signs of unauthorized access or other malicious activities. Key indicators of a cyber incident can include unusual outbound network traffic, spikes in data access or usage, alerts from intrusion detection systems, or reports of phishing attempts.

The Process of Identifying

- Effective Monitoring Systems: Implementing effective monitoring systems that can analyze network traffic and system logs for unusual activities is a critical first step in identifying cyber incidents.

- Regular Vulnerability Assessments: Conducting regular vulnerability assessments and penetration testing helps in identifying potential weaknesses that could be exploited in an attack.

- Employee Vigilance: Training employees to recognize signs of a cyber incident, such as suspicious emails or system performance issues, is also crucial in early detection.

Developing a Cyber Incident Response Plan

An effective response to a cyber incident requires a well-defined plan. This plan should outline the procedures for responding to various types of cyber incidents, detailing the roles and responsibilities of the response team, communication protocols, and steps for containing and mitigating the incident.

- Incident Response Team: Establish a dedicated incident response team with clearly defined roles. This team is responsible for managing the response to a cyber incident, from initial identification to resolution.

- Response Procedures: Develop detailed response procedures for different types of incidents. These procedures should include steps for containing the incident, eradicating the threat, recovering systems, and communicating with stakeholders.

Containing the Incident

Once a cyber incident is identified, the immediate priority is to contain it. Containment strategies may vary depending on the type of incident but generally involve isolating affected systems to prevent the spread of the threat and stopping unauthorized access.

- Isolation of Affected Systems: Quickly isolate affected systems or networks to prevent the spread of the incident. This may involve disconnecting systems from the network or shutting down certain systems.

- Limiting User Access: Temporarily restrict user access to affected systems to prevent further exploitation of vulnerabilities.

Eradicating the Threat and Recovery

After containing the incident, the focus shifts to eradicating the threat and recovering affected systems. This involves removing malware, applying patches to vulnerabilities, and restoring data from backups.

- Removal of Malicious Components: Utilize cybersecurity tools to remove malware or other malicious components from the organization's systems.

- Applying Security Patches: Apply patches to any vulnerabilities that were exploited in the incident.

- System Recovery: Restore affected systems and data from backups, ensuring that they are free from any threats.

Effective communication is critical during and after a cyber incident. This involves internal communication within the organization and external communication with stakeholders, such as customers, partners, and regulatory bodies.

- Internal Communication: Keep relevant internal stakeholders informed about the incident and the steps being taken to address it.

- External Communication: Communicate with external stakeholders, including customers and regulatory bodies, as appropriate. Transparency is key, but it is also important to balance this with the need to protect sensitive information.

After resolving a cyber incident, conducting a post-incident analysis is vital. This analysis should review how the incident occurred, the effectiveness of the response, and lessons learned. The insights gained from this analysis should be used to improve the organization's cybersecurity posture and incident response plan.

Forensics and Investigation of Cyber Crimes

As criminal activities increasingly shift to the digital realm, the ability to uncover, analyze, and use digital evidence becomes essential for law enforcement and cybersecurity experts. Cyber forensics involves the collection, preservation, analysis, and presentation of evidence from digital sources for the purpose of investigation and legal proceedings. This discipline applies to a wide range of cyber crimes, including hacking, identity theft, online fraud, and the distribution of illegal digital content.

The Process of Digital Forensic Investigation

The process of digital forensic investigation typically involves several key stages:

- Identification: This initial stage involves identifying the source of the cyber crime or security breach. This could be a compromised computer system, a network, or a specific digital device.

- Preservation: Once the source is identified, the next step is to preserve the evidence. This involves securely collecting and storing digital data to prevent tampering or loss. Techniques like creating digital copies or images of storage devices are commonly used.

- Analysis: The analysis phase is where the collected data is scrutinized to uncover relevant information. This may involve recovering deleted files, decrypting encrypted data, or analyzing internet logs. The objective is to piece together how the cyber crime was committed and potentially identify the perpetrator.

- Documentation and Reporting: Maintaining a clear record of the forensic process and findings is essential. This documentation can be used in legal proceedings to demonstrate how the evidence was obtained and analyzed.

- Presentation: The final stage involves presenting the findings of the investigation. This could be in a court of law or to an organization's management team. The presentation must clearly convey the technical details of the cyber crime in a manner that is understandable to non-technical audiences.

Cyber forensics utilizes a variety of tools and techniques. These range from software programs that can analyze internet traffic and recover deleted files, to specialized hardware for duplicating hard drives. The field is continually evolving, with new tools being developed to keep pace with the changing nature of technology and cyber crimes.

Today, cyber forensics faces several unique challenges:

- Rapid Evolution of Technology: The rapid evolution of technology means that forensic experts must continuously update their skills and tools.

- Encryption and Anonymity: Advanced encryption methods and anonymity tools used by cybercriminals can make it challenging to retrieve and analyze data.

- Volume of Data: The sheer volume of data and the complexity of modern information systems can make the process of data analysis time-consuming and resource-intensive.

- Legal and Ethical Considerations: Ensuring that digital evidence is collected and handled in a manner that is legally admissible and ethically sound is crucial. This includes considerations like maintaining the chain of custody and respecting privacy laws.

In law enforcement, cyber forensics plays a vital role in both the detection and prosecution of crimes. Digital evidence can be key in identifying suspects, understanding the modus operandi, and providing conclusive proof in court.

The field of cyber forensics is continuously evolving. Future trends may include greater use of artificial intelligence and machine learning for data analysis, advanced techniques for decrypting data, and enhanced methods for combating the use of anonymizing technologies by cybercriminals.

Reporting Cyber Incidents: Protocols and Procedures

The protocols and procedures for reporting cyber incidents are as crucial as the measures taken to prevent them. Timely and effective reporting can significantly mitigate the damage caused by cyber incidents and is often a regulatory requirement for many organizations.

The prompt reporting of cyber incidents is essential for several reasons. It enables organizations to quickly mobilize their response teams to contain and mitigate the impact of the incident. It also facilitates the collection and preservation of evidence for forensic analysis and legal proceedings. Additionally, in many jurisdictions, there are legal obligations to report certain types of cyber incidents, particularly those involving data breaches and theft of sensitive information.

Developing a Cyber Incident Reporting Protocol

An effective cyber incident reporting protocol provides a structured approach for reporting and managing incidents. It outlines the processes for internal and external communication during and after a cyber incident.

- Identification of Reportable Incidents: The protocol should clearly define what constitutes a reportable cyber incident. This can range from data breaches and system intrusions to the detection of malware and unauthorized access to sensitive information.

- Internal Reporting Procedures: Establish clear internal reporting lines. Employees should know whom to report to in the event of detecting a potential cyber incident. This typically involves notifying the organization's cybersecurity team or IT department.

- External Reporting Obligations: Understand the legal and regulatory requirements for external reporting. This may involve notifying regulatory bodies, law enforcement agencies, affected customers, or the public.

Steps in Reporting Cyber Incidents

1. Initial Assessment and Notification: Perform an initial assessment of the incident to understand its nature and scope. Promptly notify the designated internal team or individual responsible for managing cyber incidents.

2. Documentation: Document all aspects of the incident, including how it was discovered, the suspected cause, and the potential impact. Maintaining detailed records is crucial for subsequent investigations and legal compliance.

3. Containment and Eradication: While the reporting process is underway, steps should be taken to contain and eradicate the threat, preventing further damage.

4. Communication with Stakeholders: Communicate with stakeholders, including employees, customers, and partners, as appropriate. The nature and extent of communication may depend on the severity of the incident and legal requirements.

5. Post-Incident Reporting and Review: After the incident has been contained and managed, a detailed report should be prepared. This report should include a comprehensive analysis of the incident, the effectiveness of the response, and recommendations for preventing future incidents.

Challenges

- Determining the Scope of Reporting: Deciding the extent of internal and external reporting can be challenging, especially in incidents where the full impact is not immediately clear.

- Balancing Transparency and Confidentiality: Striking a balance between being transparent about the incident and protecting sensitive information is often complex.

- Timely Reporting: Reporting incidents in a timely manner, while ensuring that the information is accurate and complete, can be challenging, especially in rapidly evolving situations.

Best Practices in Cyber Incident Reporting

- Regular Training and Awareness: Conduct regular training for employees on the importance of reporting cyber incidents and the procedures to follow.

- Clear Communication Channels: Establish and maintain clear channels for reporting incidents, both internally and externally.

- Regular Review and Updates of Reporting Protocols: Keep the incident reporting protocol updated in line with emerging threats, technological changes, and regulatory updates.

- Collaboration with External Agencies: Develop relationships with relevant external agencies, such as law enforcement and regulatory bodies, to facilitate effective reporting and response.

Recovering from Cyber Attacks

Recovery from a cyber attack involves not only restoring systems and data to their pre-attack state but also learning from the incident to bolster defenses against future attacks. Having a robust recovery plan is as crucial as preventive measures. The immediate response to a cyber attack is pivotal in minimizing its impact. This typically involves containing the attack to prevent further damage, assessing the scope and nature of the breach, and initiating the recovery process. Quick and decisive actions are crucial at this stage to limit the extent of the damage.

Understanding the full extent of the damage caused by a cyber attack is the first step in the recovery process. This involves identifying which systems, data, and networks have been affected. It's essential to determine the nature of the data compromised, whether it's confidential client information, proprietary business data, or sensitive personal employee data.

Restoring Systems and Data

Restoring systems and data is the most critical phase of the recovery process. This usually involves:

- Using Backups: Restoring data from backups is often the quickest way to regain access to affected information. It's crucial that these backups are recent and have not been compromised by the attack.

- Repairing Damaged Systems: In some cases, systems may need to be repaired or rebuilt. This might include reinstalling operating systems, applications, and security software.

- Patching Vulnerabilities: If the attack exploited specific vulnerabilities, it's vital to patch these security holes to prevent future breaches.

Communicating with Stakeholders

Effective communication during the recovery process is vital. This involves keeping internal stakeholders, such as employees and management, informed about the recovery progress. Additionally, if customer data was compromised, organizations are often legally obliged to inform affected parties. Transparent and timely communication can help maintain trust and mitigate reputational damage.

Reviewing and Learning from the Incident

Once recovery is underway or completed, it's crucial to conduct a thorough review of the incident. This should involve analyzing how the attack occurred, the effectiveness of the response, and any shortcomings in existing security measures. Insights gained from this review are essential for strengthening the organization's cybersecurity posture.

- Post-Incident Analysis: Conduct a detailed analysis of the attack to understand its origin, method, and impact. This often involves working with cybersecurity experts or forensic investigators.

- Updating Security Policies and Practices: Based on the findings of the analysis, update security policies, practices, and infrastructure as needed to prevent similar attacks in the future.

- Training and Awareness: Reinforce training and awareness programs for employees to ensure they are aware of new threats and the lessons learned from the incident.

Best Practices in Recovery Planning

- Comprehensive Recovery Plan: Have a comprehensive and tested recovery plan in place. This plan should include detailed procedures for data restoration, system repairs, and communication strategies.

- Regular Backup and Testing: Maintain regular and secure backups of all critical data and test the restoration process to ensure it works effectively.

- Cyber Insurance: Consider investing in cyber insurance to mitigate the financial impact of cyber attacks.

Recovering from a cyber attack presents several challenges, including managing the cost of recovery, dealing with operational disruptions, and handling legal and regulatory implications. The complexity of these challenges depends on the scale of the attack and the organization's preparedness.

Learning from Cyber Incidents

Each incident provides valuable insights into vulnerabilities and shortcomings in security systems, policies, and practices. Organizations that effectively analyze and learn from these incidents can significantly enhance their resilience against future threats. These lessons can guide organizations in fortifying their defenses, refining their response strategies, and developing a more proactive approach to cybersecurity. Failure to learn from these incidents can leave organizations vulnerable to repeat occurrences and potentially more severe consequences.

Conducting a Post-Incident Analysis

A comprehensive post-incident analysis is key to extracting valuable lessons from a cyber incident. This process typically involves several steps:

- Detailed Incident Review: Conduct a thorough review of the incident to understand its causes and impact. This includes examining how the incident occurred, the entry points used, and the vulnerabilities exploited.

- Assessment of Response Effectiveness: Evaluate the effectiveness of the organization's response to the incident. This involves analyzing the speed and efficiency of the response, the decision-making process, and the coordination among different teams.

- Identification of Security Gaps: Identify any gaps or weaknesses in the organization's cybersecurity measures that were exposed by the incident. This could include technical vulnerabilities, inadequate policies, or lack of employee awareness.

The insights gained from the post-incident analysis should be translated into actionable improvements. This involves:

- Updating Security Measures: Strengthen security measures to address the identified vulnerabilities. This may involve updating software, enhancing network security, or deploying new security technologies.

- Revising Policies and Procedures: Update organizational policies and procedures based on the lessons learned. This could include changes to access controls, incident response protocols, or data management practices.

- Training and Awareness Programs: Enhance employee training and awareness programs to address any knowledge gaps or behavioral issues that contributed to the incident.

Challenges in Learning from Cyber Incidents

- Accurate and Honest Assessment: Conducting an unbiased and thorough assessment of an incident can be challenging, particularly in identifying internal shortcomings or failures.

- Resource Constraints: Allocating the necessary resources for a comprehensive analysis and implementation of lessons can be difficult, especially for organizations with limited cybersecurity budgets.

- Complexity of Cyber Threats: The ever-evolving nature of cyber threats can make it challenging to keep up with the necessary knowledge and skills to effectively analyze and learn from incidents.

Best Practices for Maximizing Learning

- Foster a Culture of Continuous Learning: Cultivate an organizational culture that values learning from mistakes and encourages open discussion and analysis of cyber incidents.

- Collaboration and Information Sharing: Collaborate with other organizations, industry groups, and cybersecurity experts to share insights and learn from a broader range of incidents.

- Regular Reviews and Updates: Regularly review and update cybersecurity strategies and practices to reflect new learnings and evolving threats.

Legal and Ethical Aspects of Cybersecurity

Today, understanding cyber laws and regulations is imperative for individuals and organizations alike. These laws and regulations are designed to protect users online, ensure data privacy, combat cybercrime, and maintain a secure cyberspace. As cyber threats evolve, so do these legal frameworks, making it crucial for those involved in the digital domain to stay informed about current laws and their implications.

Cyber laws and regulations play a critical role in the digital world. They provide a legal framework for addressing issues that arise in the online environment, such as data breaches, unauthorized access, cyberbullying, identity theft, and intellectual property disputes. For businesses, these laws ensure that they handle customer data responsibly and protect it from cyber threats. Failure to comply with these laws can lead to significant legal, financial, and reputational consequences.

Key Areas Covered by Cyber Laws

- Data Protection and Privacy: Laws in this area, such as the General Data Protection Regulation (GDPR) in the European Union, regulate how personal data is collected, used, and protected. They mandate certain protections for data and give individuals rights over their personal information.

- Intellectual Property: Cyber laws protect digital intellectual property rights, covering areas such as copyright, trademarks, and patents in the digital space.

- Cybercrime: These laws deal with criminal activities conducted online, including hacking, identity theft, phishing, and the distribution of malware.

- E-commerce: Laws regulating online business transactions ensure the legality of contracts, consumer rights, and fair trade practices in the digital marketplace.

Impact on Organizations

For organizations, compliance with cyber laws is not optional but a mandatory aspect of their operations. This involves:

- Implementing Data Protection Measures: Organizations must implement robust data protection measures to comply with privacy laws. This includes securing customer data against unauthorized access and breaches.

- Reporting Obligations: Many regulations require organizations to report data breaches within a specified timeframe. Failure to do so can result in hefty fines and penalties.

- User Consent and Transparency: Organizations must ensure transparent data practices, often requiring explicit user consent for data collection and use.

Cyber laws vary significantly across different jurisdictions, presenting a challenge for global businesses. Organizations operating internationally must navigate a complex web of laws that may differ from one country to another.

As technology advances, cyber laws continually evolve to address new challenges and threats. This dynamic nature requires organizations and individuals to stay informed about the latest legal developments in their jurisdictions and globally.

Compliance with cyber laws can be challenging, particularly for smaller organizations with limited resources. The complexity of laws, especially in a cross-border context, adds to the compliance burden. Organizations often need to invest in legal expertise, cybersecurity tools, and training to ensure compliance.

Best Practices for Compliance

- Regular Training and Awareness: Educate employees regularly about the importance of cyber laws and the organization's policies for compliance.

- Stay Informed: Keep abreast of changes and updates in cyber laws and regulations. This may involve consulting with legal experts specializing in cyber law.

- Implement a Compliance Framework: Develop and implement a compliance framework that includes policies, procedures, and tools aligned with legal requirements.

- Data Governance and Management: Establish effective data governance and management practices to ensure data is handled in compliance with legal requirements.

Ethical Hacking: The White Hat Professionals

Ethical hacking has emerged as a vital practice for strengthening system security. Ethical hackers, also known as white hat hackers, are professionals who utilize their skills to identify and fix vulnerabilities in computer systems. Unlike malicious hackers, who exploit weaknesses for personal gain, ethical hackers work with organizations to improve their defenses against cyber attacks.

Ethical hackers play a critical role in the cybersecurity ecosystem. They use the same techniques and tools as malicious hackers but do so legally and ethically to help organizations bolster their security. By thinking like a hacker, they can better anticipate and mitigate potential attacks. Their work is crucial in identifying vulnerabilities that could be exploited and recommending measures to rectify these weaknesses.

Key Methodologies in Ethical Hacking

Ethical hacking involves a variety of methodologies, all aimed at assessing the security of computer systems:

- Penetration Testing: This is one of the primary methods used by ethical hackers. It involves attempting to breach the security of systems and networks to identify vulnerabilities. Penetration tests can be performed with different scopes and objectives, ranging from testing specific systems to attempting to access sensitive data.

- Vulnerability Assessment: Unlike penetration testing, which tries to exploit vulnerabilities, vulnerability assessments focus on identifying potential vulnerabilities in a system or network. This includes scanning for known vulnerabilities and misconfigurations.

- Social Engineering: This technique involves manipulating individuals into divulging sensitive information or performing actions that compromise security. Ethical hackers use social engineering tests to assess the human element of cybersecurity.

Ethical hacking is governed by strict legal and ethical guidelines. Ethical hackers must have explicit permission from the organization to test their systems. They are also bound by confidentiality agreements to protect the sensitive data they access during their work. Additionally, ethical hackers must ensure that their actions do not harm the systems they are testing.

In an environment where cyber threats are constantly evolving, ethical hacking is essential for:

- Proactive Security: By identifying and addressing vulnerabilities before they can be exploited, ethical hacking allows organizations to adopt a proactive approach to cybersecurity.

- Keeping Pace with Cyber Threats: As cyber threats become more sophisticated, ethical hacking helps organizations stay one step ahead of malicious attackers.

- Building Trust and Credibility: Organizations that engage in ethical hacking demonstrate a commitment to security, thereby building trust among customers and stakeholders.

Becoming an ethical hacker requires a blend of technical skills, creativity, and ethical judgment. Prospective ethical hackers often need extensive knowledge in areas such as networking, programming, and information security. Many ethical hackers hold certifications like the Certified Ethical Hacker (CEH) or Offensive Security Certified Professional (OSCP).

Challenges Faced by Ethical Hackers

Ethical hackers often face unique challenges, such as:

- Keeping Skills Up-to-Date: With rapidly evolving technology and cyber threats, ethical hackers must continuously update their skills and knowledge.

- Balancing Offensive and Defensive Tactics: Ethical hackers must balance offensive tactics (like penetration testing) with defensive strategies (like vulnerability management).

- Navigating Legal and Ethical Boundaries: Ensuring that all activities are within legal and ethical boundaries is crucial for maintaining professional integrity.

Data Protection Laws and Compliance

Data protection laws have become increasingly significant, driven by the rising concerns over privacy and security of personal data. Compliance with these laws is not just a legal necessity but also a crucial aspect of building trust and maintaining the integrity of organizations.

Data protection laws are designed to safeguard personal information against misuse and unauthorized access. The evolution of these laws can be attributed to the exponential growth of digital data and the proliferation of technologies that collect and process personal information. These laws regulate how personal data should be collected, processed, stored, and shared.

Key Data Protection Regulations

General Data Protection Regulation (GDPR): Enacted by the European Union, GDPR is one of the most comprehensive data protection regulations globally. It provides individuals with greater control over their personal data and imposes strict rules on data processing for organizations operating within and outside the EU.

California Consumer Privacy Act (CCPA): CCPA is a state statute intended to enhance privacy rights and consumer protection for residents of California, USA. It provides California residents with the right to know about the personal data collected about them and the purpose of its collection.

Other Regional Laws: Many other countries and regions have implemented their data protection laws, such as the Personal Data Protection Act (PDPA) in Singapore and the Data Protection Act in the UK.

Principles of Data Protection

Data protection laws typically revolve around several key principles:

- Lawfulness, Fairness, and Transparency: Personal data must be processed lawfully, fairly, and in a transparent manner.

- Purpose Limitation: Data should be collected for specified, explicit, and legitimate purposes and not further processed in a manner incompatible with those purposes.

- Data Minimization: The collection of personal data should be adequate, relevant, and limited to what is necessary in relation to the purposes for which they are processed.

- Accuracy: Personal data should be accurate and, where necessary, kept up to date.

- Storage Limitation: Personal data should be kept in a form that permits identification of data subjects for no longer than is necessary for the purposes for which the personal data are processed.

- Integrity and Confidentiality: Personal data should be processed in a manner that ensures appropriate security, including protection against unauthorized or unlawful processing and accidental loss, destruction, or damage.

The Importance of Compliance

- Compliance with data protection laws is vital for several reasons:

- Legal Obligations: Non-compliance can result in significant penalties and legal repercussions.

- Reputation and Trust: Organizations that adhere to data protection laws are more likely to be trusted by customers and partners.

- Risk Management: Compliance helps in mitigating risks associated with data breaches and the misuse of personal information.

Achieving compliance can be challenging, particularly for organizations that operate across multiple jurisdictions or handle large volumes of data. These challenges include keeping up-to-date with changing regulations, implementing comprehensive data protection policies, and ensuring continuous enforcement of these policies.

Best Practices for Ensuring Compliance

- Regular Audits and Assessments: Conduct regular audits to assess compliance with data protection laws.

- Data Protection Officer (DPO): Appoint a DPO or a similar role responsible for overseeing data protection strategy and compliance.

- Employee Training: Regularly train employees on the importance of data protection and the procedures to follow.

- Data Processing Records: Maintain detailed records of data processing activities.

- Incident Response Plan: Develop a robust incident response plan to deal with data breaches effectively.

Ethical Considerations in Cybersecurity

As cybersecurity professionals navigate the complex landscape of protecting digital assets, they must constantly weigh their actions and decisions against a backdrop of ethical principles.

The Ethical Dimension of Cybersecurity

At its core, cybersecurity is about protecting information and systems from unauthorized access and harm. This responsibility carries with it an inherent set of ethical considerations, as actions taken in the name of security can have significant implications for privacy, individual rights, and organizational integrity. Cybersecurity professionals must balance the need to secure systems with respect for user privacy and data protection.

Privacy and Data Protection

One of the primary ethical considerations in cybersecurity is the respect for user privacy and the protection of personal data. Cybersecurity measures should be designed to protect user data from unauthorized access while also respecting the privacy rights of individuals. This involves careful consideration of what data is collected, how it is stored, and who has access to it.

- Consent and Transparency: Users should be informed about the data being collected and its purpose. Consent should be obtained wherever necessary, especially for sensitive information.

- Minimization of Data Collection: Collect only the data that is necessary for the intended purpose, avoiding unnecessary data collection that could infringe on privacy.

Balancing Security and User Freedom

Cybersecurity measures should not unnecessarily infringe on user freedoms or create an environment of undue surveillance. Striking a balance between effective security and the maintenance of an open, free digital environment is a key ethical challenge.

- Proportionality of Measures: Security measures should be proportional to the threat, avoiding excessive restrictions or controls that could impede user freedoms.

- Avoiding Overreach: Cybersecurity practices should not overreach into areas that infringe on personal liberties or privacy without clear justification and legal backing.

- Transparency and Honesty: In the event of a data breach, organizations have an ethical obligation to be transparent and inform affected parties promptly.

- Ethical Response to Cyber Attacks: Responses to cyber attacks should be ethical and legal. Actions such as counter-attacking or hacking back are often legally dubious and ethically questionable.

The Responsibility of Cybersecurity Professionals

Cybersecurity professionals bear a significant responsibility to act ethically, given their access to sensitive systems and data.

- Adherence to Professional Codes of Conduct: Many cybersecurity professionals are bound by codes of conduct set by professional organizations, which outline ethical practices and responsibilities.

- Continuous Ethical Education: Staying informed about ethical issues in cybersecurity and ongoing education are important for professionals to navigate the evolving ethical landscape.

International Cooperation in Cybersecurity

Cybersecurity challenges such as cross-border data breaches, international cybercrime, and state-sponsored cyber attacks require a concerted and coordinated response from nations around the world. Cyber threats often originate from and impact multiple countries, transcending national jurisdictions. As such, no single nation can effectively combat these threats in isolation. International cooperation facilitates the sharing of information, resources, and best practices, enhancing the ability of nations to protect against and respond to cyber threats effectively.

Mechanisms for International Cooperation

- Bilateral and Multilateral Agreements: Countries often enter into bilateral or multilateral agreements to collaborate on cybersecurity matters. These agreements can include commitments to share threat intelligence, collaborate on law enforcement efforts, or engage in joint research and development.

- Global Cybersecurity Alliances: Organizations like the European Union Agency for Cybersecurity (ENISA), the Council of Europe's Budapest Convention on Cybercrime, and the Global Forum on Cyber Expertise (GFCE) provide platforms for nations to collaborate on cybersecurity initiatives.

- Information Sharing Networks: International networks and alliances facilitate the exchange of cybersecurity information and intelligence. Examples include the Computer Emergency Response Teams (CERTs) and Information Sharing and Analysis Centers (ISACs) that operate across various sectors and regions.

Challenges in International Cybersecurity

Despite its importance, international cooperation in cybersecurity faces several challenges:

- Differing National Laws and Policies: Variations in national cybersecurity laws and policies can impede cooperation. For instance, what is considered lawful and ethical in one country may be viewed differently in another.

- Sovereignty Concerns: Nations may be reluctant to share sensitive information or collaborate on cybersecurity initiatives due to concerns over sovereignty and national security.

- Resource Disparities: There is often a disparity in cybersecurity capabilities and resources among countries, which can affect the efficacy of cooperative efforts.

- Political and Diplomatic Challenges: Political and diplomatic relations between countries can impact their willingness and ability to cooperate on cybersecurity issues.

To overcome these challenges and strengthen international cooperation in cybersecurity, several steps can be taken:

- Harmonization of Cybersecurity Laws and Policies: Efforts to harmonize cybersecurity laws and policies can facilitate more effective cooperation. This could involve establishing international cybersecurity standards or guidelines.

- Building Trust: Developing trust among nations is crucial for effective cooperation. This can be achieved through regular dialogue, joint exercises, and transparency in cybersecurity practices.

- Capacity Building: Assisting countries with limited cybersecurity capabilities through training, technical support, and resource sharing can help create a more balanced and effective cooperative environment.

- Engagement in International Forums: Active participation in international forums and organizations dedicated to cybersecurity can help nations stay engaged in global discussions and initiatives.

In addition to governmental efforts, non-governmental actors, including international organizations, private sector companies, and academia, play a vital role in promoting international cooperation in cybersecurity. Their expertise, resources, and perspectives can significantly contribute to the development and implementation of global cybersecurity strategies.

Building a Cybersecurity Career

The cybersecurity field is rapidly evolving, requiring a continuous influx of skilled professionals. The educational pathways into this dynamic field are varied and adaptable, catering to individuals with diverse interests and career aspirations.

Traditional Academic Routes

Universities and colleges globally are recognizing the growing need for cybersecurity expertise, resulting in specialized degree programs. These range from associate degrees to doctoral studies, encompassing a breadth of topics like network security, information assurance, ethical hacking, and cryptography. Bachelor's programs lay a foundational understanding of cybersecurity principles, while graduate degrees delve into advanced and often specialized topics in the field.

Professional Certifications

Professional certifications hold significant value in the cybersecurity realm, demonstrating specialized knowledge and practical skills. Certifications such as the Certified Information Systems Security Professional (CISSP) are recognized globally and cater to experienced professionals. Others like the Certified Ethical Hacker (CEH) and

CompTIA Security+ are tailored to individuals at different stages of their cybersecurity careers, focusing on ethical hacking skills and foundational cybersecurity knowledge, respectively.

Skills-Based and Vocational Training

For those seeking a more hands-on and practical approach, vocational courses and bootcamps present an effective alternative. These programs are typically shorter and more intensive, focusing directly on the skills required in the cybersecurity workforce. Cybersecurity bootcamps, ranging from a few weeks to several months, combine theoretical learning with practical experience. Additionally, online courses and Massive Open Online Courses (MOOCs) offer flexible learning opportunities, often developed by universities or industry experts.

Continuous Learning and Specialization

Given the fast-paced evolution of cybersecurity threats and technologies, continuous learning is a non-negotiable aspect of a cybersecurity professional's career. Professionals in the field often choose to specialize in specific areas such as network security, cloud security, or cyber law and policy. Engaging in regular workshops, seminars, and conferences is also crucial for staying updated with the latest trends and advancements in the field.

Developing Soft Skills

In cybersecurity, technical acumen needs to be complemented with strong soft skills. Problem-solving abilities are paramount in addressing complex cybersecurity challenges. Effective communication skills are essential for articulating complex cybersecurity concepts to non-technical stakeholders. Furthermore, the sensitive nature of cybersecurity work demands a solid foundation in ethical judgment.

Key Skills and Competencies

As cyber threats grow in complexity and sophistication, professionals in this field must equip themselves with a diverse set of abilities.

Technical Proficiency in Cybersecurity

The cornerstone of a cybersecurity professional's skill set is deep technical knowledge, which includes but is not limited to:

1. Understanding of Networks and Systems: A thorough grasp of how networks and systems operate is fundamental. This includes knowledge of network architectures, protocols, and various operating systems. Professionals must understand how data moves within and between networks and the potential vulnerabilities in these processes.

2. Proficiency in Security Technologies: Familiarity with a range of security technologies, such as firewalls, intrusion detection systems, anti-virus software, and encryption tools, is essential. Knowing how to deploy, manage, and troubleshoot these technologies forms a significant part of a cybersecurity professional's role.

3. Awareness of Current Threat Landscape: Keeping abreast of the current threat landscape, including the latest types of cyberattacks and emerging threats, is vital. This requires continuous learning and research.

4. Incident Response and Recovery Skills: Skills in incident response and recovery are crucial. Professionals must know how to respond to a security breach, limit damage, and restore normal operations as quickly as possible.

5. Knowledge of Compliance and Legal Requirements: Understanding the legal and compliance aspects of information security is critical. This includes familiarity with laws and regulations like GDPR, HIPAA, and others that impact data security and privacy.

Analytical and Problem-Solving Skills

Cybersecurity is a field driven by problem-solving. Professionals must possess:

1. Analytical Thinking: The ability to analyze vast amounts of data and identify patterns is crucial. Cybersecurity professionals often deal with complex systems and networks, where they need to quickly identify the root cause of security issues.

2. Creative Problem-Solving: Cyber threats are often novel and unexpected. Professionals must think creatively to develop innovative solutions to safeguard against these threats.

3. Decision-Making Abilities: In many instances, cybersecurity professionals must make quick decisions about how to best protect systems. This requires the ability to assess risks and make sound judgments under pressure.

Communication and Collaboration

1. Clear Communication: Professionals must articulate complex cybersecurity concepts clearly and effectively to both technical and non-technical stakeholders. This also includes writing comprehensive reports and documentation.

2. Collaboration Skills: Cybersecurity is often a team effort. Professionals need to work collaboratively with other IT staff, management, and sometimes external agencies.

3. Teaching and Mentoring Abilities: As cybersecurity is a continuously evolving field, professionals should be able to educate and mentor others within their organizations about best security practices.

Soft Skills

In addition to technical abilities, several soft skills are indispensable:

1. Adaptability and Flexibility: The ability to adapt to rapidly changing scenarios and technologies is crucial in cybersecurity.

2. Attention to Detail: Small oversights can lead to significant security breaches. Therefore, meticulous attention to detail is necessary.

3. Ethical Integrity: Cybersecurity professionals often have access to sensitive information. Maintaining high ethical standards and confidentiality is imperative.

4. Resilience and Stress Management: Given the high stakes involved, the ability to handle stress and bounce back from challenging situations is crucial.

Leadership and Management Skills

For those aspiring to lead cybersecurity teams or departments, additional skills are needed:

1. Strategic Planning: The ability to develop and implement comprehensive security strategies is key.

2. People Management: Skills in managing and leading teams, including conflict resolution, motivation, and performance management, are important.

3. Budgeting and Resource Allocation: Understanding how to allocate resources effectively and manage budgets is crucial for cybersecurity leaders.

Career Opportunities in Cybersecurity

As technology continues to advance and integrate into every aspect of life and business, the importance of securing digital assets and information becomes paramount. This has led to a burgeoning demand for cybersecurity professionals across a wide range of industries, including government, finance, healthcare, retail, and technology.

Core Cybersecurity Roles

- Cybersecurity Analyst: This role involves monitoring and analyzing an organization's security posture and defending against cyber threats. Analysts assess security systems, identify vulnerabilities, and recommend enhancements to prevent data breaches.

- Security Architect: A security architect is responsible for designing robust security structures to protect an organization's computer systems and networks. This role requires a deep understanding of IT systems, networks, and security protocols.

- Penetration Tester (Ethical Hacker): Penetration testers simulate cyber-attacks to identify vulnerabilities in security systems before malicious hackers can exploit them. This role requires a mix of creativity, technical skills, and a deep understanding of cyber threats and hacking techniques.

- Incident Responder: Incident responders are the first line of defense when a cybersecurity breach occurs. They manage the situation to minimize damage, analyze the breach, and plan recovery steps.

- Chief Information Security Officer (CISO): The CISO is a senior-level executive responsible for an organization's overall security strategy, ensuring that cybersecurity policies and procedures are aligned with business objectives.

Specialized Cybersecurity Careers

- Cybersecurity Consultant: Consultants provide expert advice to organizations on how to protect their IT infrastructure from cyber threats. This role often involves assessing existing security measures, identifying vulnerabilities, and recommending solutions.

- Forensic Computer Analyst: These professionals are involved in investigating cybercrimes and analyzing breaches. They gather and evaluate evidence from computers, networks, and data storage devices to trace and rectify the source of attacks.

- Information Security Analyst: Focused on protecting an organization's sensitive and proprietary information, these analysts implement security measures and protect against unauthorized access to computer systems and data.

- Network Security Engineer: This role involves designing, implementing, and managing security measures to protect an organization's network and systems.

- Compliance and Risk Management: Professionals in this area focus on ensuring that cybersecurity policies and procedures comply with regulatory standards and help in managing organizational risk.

Emerging Areas in Cybersecurity

- Cloud Security Specialist: With the shift towards cloud computing, specialists in cloud security are increasingly in demand. They are responsible for securing cloud-based platforms and managing cloud security risks.

- IoT Security Specialist: As the Internet of Things (IoT) becomes more prevalent, security specialists in this area focus on securing interconnected devices and networks.

- AI Security Specialist: With the integration of AI in cybersecurity, specialists in this area focus on using artificial intelligence to enhance security protocols and counter sophisticated cyber threats.

Entering the cybersecurity field typically requires a combination of education, certifications, and practical experience. Many professionals start with a degree in computer science, information technology, or cybersecurity. Certifications like Certified Information Systems Security Professional (CISSP) or Certified Ethical Hacker (CEH) are also beneficial. Practical experience, which can be gained through internships, entry-level IT roles, or even personal projects, is invaluable.

Networking and Community Involvement

Networking and community involvement have become indispensable tools for professionals looking to grow their careers, stay informed about the latest trends, and contribute to the broader cybersecurity community. In a domain where sharing knowledge and experiences is key to combating emerging threats, these practices are not just beneficial; they are essential.

Networking in cybersecurity goes beyond the conventional notion of building professional contacts. It is about creating a web of relationships with peers, mentors, industry leaders, and newcomers. These connections provide a platform for exchanging ideas, learning about the latest technological advancements, and staying updated with new threats and solutions.

- Knowledge Sharing and Learning: In an industry characterized by rapid changes and evolving threats, staying informed is crucial. Networking allows professionals to share knowledge and learn from the experiences of others. This can include insights into tackling specific security challenges, advice on career development, and information about emerging technologies.

- Career Development: Networking can open doors to new career opportunities in cybersecurity. It often leads to mentorship opportunities, job offers, and collaborations on projects or research. Building a strong professional network can be a significant asset in advancing one's career.

- Collaboration and Support: Cybersecurity professionals often face complex challenges that require collaborative efforts to solve. Networking provides a platform for professionals to collaborate on projects, share resources, and offer support to each other in tackling difficult security issues.

Being an active member of the cybersecurity community is about more than just building individual knowledge and career advancement. It involves contributing to the growth and development of the field as a whole.

- Participation in Conferences and Workshops: Attending and participating in cybersecurity conferences, workshops, and seminars is a great way to engage with the community. These events offer opportunities to learn from keynote speakers, participate in workshops, and engage in discussions about the latest trends and challenges in the field.

- Contributing to Online Forums and Platforms: Online communities and forums offer another avenue for engagement. Participating in discussions, answering questions, and sharing experiences on platforms such as Reddit, LinkedIn groups, or specialized cybersecurity forums can help in building a presence in the cybersecurity community.

- Engaging in Collaborative Research and Projects: Working on collaborative research projects or contributing to open-source cybersecurity initiatives can be highly rewarding. These projects not only contribute to the advancement of the field but also offer opportunities to work with diverse groups of professionals.

- Mentorship and Advocacy: Experienced professionals can give back to the community by mentoring newcomers or advocating for important issues in cybersecurity. This can involve guiding young professionals, speaking at educational institutions, or participating in initiatives aimed at promoting cybersecurity awareness.

Building a Strong Network

Building a strong network in cybersecurity involves a proactive approach:

- Be Active in Professional Associations: Joining professional associations such as ISACA, (ISC)², or local cybersecurity groups can provide valuable networking opportunities.

- Leverage Social Media: Social media platforms can be powerful tools for networking. Engaging with cybersecurity topics on LinkedIn, Twitter, and other platforms can help in building connections and staying informed.

- Attend Industry Events: Regularly attending industry events, meetups, and workshops is an effective way to meet peers and leaders in the field.

- Volunteer: Volunteering for cybersecurity events or community initiatives can be a great way to meet like-minded professionals and contribute to the community.

Future of Cybersecurity

Emerging Technologies: AI and Machine Learning

In the domain of cybersecurity, the advent of Artificial Intelligence (AI) and Machine Learning (ML) has ushered in a new era of possibilities and challenges. As cyber threats become increasingly sophisticated, the integration of AI and ML into cybersecurity strategies offers significant potential to enhance defense mechanisms.

AI and ML are at the forefront of technological innovation in cybersecurity. AI refers to the capability of a machine to imitate intelligent human behavior, while ML is a subset of AI that enables systems to learn and improve from experience without being explicitly programmed. In cybersecurity, these technologies are employed to predict, detect, and respond to cyber threats with a level of efficiency and speed that is challenging for humans to match.

Enhanced Threat Detection

One of the primary applications of AI and ML in cybersecurity is in the detection of threats and anomalies. By analyzing vast amounts of data, AI algorithms can identify patterns and behaviors indicative of cyber threats, such as malware attacks, phishing attempts, or unauthorized intrusions.

- Pattern Recognition: ML algorithms can be trained to recognize patterns and anomalies in network traffic, user behavior, and application performance, flagging activities that deviate from the norm.

- Predictive Analysis: AI systems can predict potential vulnerabilities and threat vectors by analyzing historical data and identifying trends.

Automated Response to Incidents

AI and ML can automate the response to cybersecurity incidents, thereby reducing the time between threat detection and response.

- Automated Remediation: AI-driven systems can automatically contain and remediate detected threats, reducing the reliance on manual intervention and accelerating the response time.

- Incident Analysis: ML algorithms can assist in analyzing past incidents to identify the root cause and prevent similar attacks in the future.

Challenges in AI and ML Implementation

While AI and ML offer tremendous potential in enhancing cybersecurity, their implementation comes with its set of challenges:

- Data Quality and Quantity: The effectiveness of ML algorithms largely depends on the quality and quantity of data used for training. Inaccurate or biased data can lead to false positives or missed threats.

- Complexity and Interpretability: AI and ML systems can be highly complex, making it difficult for cybersecurity professionals to understand and interpret their decisions and actions.

- Adaptive Threats: As AI and ML are increasingly used in cybersecurity, there is a risk that attackers will also use these technologies to develop more sophisticated attack methods.

Ethical Considerations and Privacy

The use of AI and ML in cybersecurity also raises ethical considerations and privacy concerns.

- Privacy Concerns: The extensive data collection required for AI and ML could infringe on individual privacy rights, necessitating careful consideration of privacy laws and regulations.

- Ethical Decision-Making: Ensuring that AI systems make ethical decisions, especially in situations involving personal data and privacy, is a significant concern.

Looking ahead, AI and ML are set to play an increasingly integral role in cybersecurity.

- Advanced Threat Intelligence: AI and ML will continue to advance threat intelligence capabilities, offering more accurate and proactive identification of emerging threats.

- Integration with Other Technologies: The integration of AI and ML with other emerging technologies like the Internet of Things (IoT) and blockchain could lead to more robust and comprehensive cybersecurity solutions.

- Continuous Learning and Adaptation: As AI and ML technologies evolve, they will become more adept at learning and adapting to new threats, potentially staying ahead of cybercriminals' tactics.

Quantum Computing in Cybersecurity

Quantum computing, a revolutionary technology based on the principles of quantum mechanics, is poised to redefine the landscape of cybersecurity. With its extraordinary computational power, quantum computing presents both unprecedented opportunities and challenges in the field of cybersecurity.

Quantum computing differs fundamentally from classical computing in its approach to data processing. While classical computers use bits (0s and 1s) for processing information, quantum computers use quantum bits or qubits. Qubits can exist in multiple states simultaneously, thanks to the quantum properties of superposition and entanglement. This allows quantum computers to perform complex calculations at speeds unattainable by traditional computers.

The advent of quantum computing is a double-edged sword in the realm of cybersecurity. On one hand, it offers powerful tools to enhance security systems; on the other, it poses significant threats, especially to current encryption standards.

- Breaking Current Encryption Standards: One of the most significant concerns is quantum computing's potential to break widely-used cryptographic algorithms. Many of today's encryption methods, including RSA and ECC (Elliptic Curve Cryptography), rely on the difficulty of factoring large numbers or solving discrete logarithm problems—tasks that quantum computers could solve much more efficiently than classical computers.

- Quantum Cryptography and Secure Communication: Conversely, quantum computing also paves the way for quantum cryptography, which can theoretically create unbreakable encryption. Quantum key distribution (QKD), for instance, uses the principles of quantum mechanics to securely distribute encryption keys, with the unique property that any attempt to intercept the key changes its state, thus revealing the presence of an eavesdropper.

Preparing for the Quantum Era

Given the potential of quantum computing to disrupt current cybersecurity practices, preparation is key.

- Development of Quantum-Resistant Algorithms: Organizations and governments are researching and developing new cryptographic algorithms resistant to quantum computing attacks. This field, known as post-quantum cryptography, aims to create encryption methods that can secure data against both classical and quantum computing threats.

- Investment in Quantum Computing Research: Investing in quantum computing research is essential to understand and harness its capabilities for cybersecurity purposes. This includes developing quantum computing hardware, software, and algorithms.

- Risk Assessment and Strategic Planning: Enterprises and governments need to assess their risk exposure to quantum computing and strategically plan to upgrade or replace vulnerable systems. This might involve updating encryption methods, redesigning network architectures, and reevaluating data security protocols.

Educational and Workforce Development

As quantum computing continues to evolve, there is a growing need for professionals skilled in this new technology.

- Specialized Education and Training: Educational institutions are beginning to offer courses and programs focused on quantum computing and its applications in cybersecurity. Ongoing training for existing cybersecurity professionals is also crucial to update their knowledge and skills.

- Collaboration between Academia and Industry: Collaborations between academic institutions and industry players can foster innovation and workforce development in quantum computing.

Challenges and Ethical Considerations

The integration of quantum computing into cybersecurity is not without challenges and ethical considerations.

- Technical Challenges: The development of stable, scalable quantum computers is still a major technical challenge. Issues such as error correction and qubit coherence need to be addressed.

- Ethical and Legal Implications: The use of quantum computing in cybersecurity raises various ethical and legal questions, particularly regarding privacy and data protection. The potential of quantum computing to decrypt currently secure communications poses significant ethical dilemmas.

Cybersecurity in an IoT World

The integration of the Internet of Things (IoT) into daily life and business operations has brought about a revolutionary change in how we interact with technology. However, this widespread adoption of IoT devices also presents significant cybersecurity challenges.

IoT refers to the network of physical devices that are connected to the internet, collecting and sharing data. This includes everything from smart home appliances and wearable fitness trackers to industrial sensors and smart city technologies. The proliferation of these devices has made life more convenient and operations more efficient. However, it also significantly expands the attack surface for cyber threats.

Cybersecurity Risks in IoT

The nature of IoT devices poses unique cybersecurity risks:

- Increased Attack Surface: Each IoT device represents a potential entry point for cyber attacks. The diversity and sheer number of these devices create a vast and often poorly secured attack surface.

- Inherent Vulnerabilities: Many IoT devices have inherent vulnerabilities due to limited processing power and storage, which restricts the implementation of robust security measures. Often, these devices are designed with functionality and convenience in mind, with security being an afterthought.

- Data Privacy Concerns: IoT devices collect vast amounts of data, some of which can be highly sensitive. The interception or unauthorized access to this data poses significant privacy risks.

- Complex Ecosystems: IoT environments often involve a complex ecosystem of devices, manufacturers, and service providers. This complexity can make it difficult to manage security effectively and to identify who is responsible for ensuring the security of the data and devices.

Strategies for Securing IoT

Addressing the cybersecurity challenges of IoT requires a multifaceted approach:

- Secure Device Design and Manufacturing: Manufacturers must prioritize security in the design and manufacturing of IoT devices. This includes embedding security features at the hardware level and ensuring that software is secure and regularly updated.

- Robust Network Security Measures: Implementing robust security measures in networks that host IoT devices is crucial. This includes network segmentation, firewalls, and intrusion detection and prevention systems.

- Regular Software Updates and Patch Management: Regularly updating the software on IoT devices is essential to protect against known vulnerabilities. Patch management should be an integral part of the IoT security strategy.

- Authentication and Access Control: Strong authentication and access control mechanisms are essential for securing IoT devices. This may involve the use of passwords, digital certificates, or biometric authentication.

- Data Encryption: Encrypting the data transmitted by IoT devices can help protect the integrity and confidentiality of the data, especially when it is being transmitted over public networks.

- Monitoring and Response: Continuous monitoring of IoT devices and networks is necessary to detect and respond to potential security incidents promptly.

Securing IoT environments presents several challenges:

- Diverse and Evolving Nature of IoT Devices: The diversity of IoT devices and the rapid pace at which they evolve make it challenging to establish standardized security protocols.

- Resource Constraints: Some IoT devices have limited processing power and storage, constraining the implementation of comprehensive security measures.

- Integration with Legacy Systems: Integrating IoT devices with existing legacy systems can create additional security vulnerabilities.

- Awareness and Education: There is often a lack of awareness about the security risks associated with IoT devices among users and manufacturers, which can lead to inadequate security practices.

Predictive Analytics

Predictive analytics in cybersecurity represents a significant shift from traditional reactive methods to a more proactive approach. Utilizing advanced analytical techniques and machine learning algorithms, predictive analytics aims to foresee and prevent cyber threats before they materialize.

Traditionally, cybersecurity has focused on reacting to threats as they occur. Predictive analytics, however, introduces the ability to anticipate threats. By analyzing patterns and trends from a vast array of data sources, cybersecurity systems can predict vulnerabilities, detect emerging threats, and prevent breaches before they happen.

Methodologies of Predictive Analytics

Predictive analytics in cybersecurity utilizes a variety of data analysis techniques:

Data Mining: This involves extracting valuable patterns and insights from large sets of data. In cybersecurity, data mining can reveal hidden patterns in network traffic, user behavior, and system logs that might indicate a potential security threat.

- Machine Learning Algorithms: Machine learning allows systems to learn from data, identify patterns, and make decisions with minimal human intervention. In cybersecurity, machine learning algorithms can be trained to detect anomalies that deviate from normal behavior, potentially flagging malicious activities.

- Behavioral Analysis: By analyzing the behavior of users and systems, predictive analytics can identify actions that deviate from the norm. This includes unusual login times, high data usage, or unexpected access to sensitive areas of a network.

- Risk Scoring Models: Predictive analytics can use risk scoring models to assess the likelihood of a threat. These models evaluate various factors like user activities, system changes, and external threats to calculate a risk score, enabling prioritized responses to the most critical threats.

Application in Cyber Defense Strategies

The application of predictive analytics in cybersecurity has several key implications:

- Anticipating Attack Strategies: Predictive analytics can help in understanding the tactics, techniques, and procedures (TTPs) of attackers, allowing organizations to anticipate and prepare for specific types of attacks.

- Enhancing Threat Intelligence: It contributes to more sophisticated threat intelligence, providing insights not only into current threats but also forecasting future cybersecurity trends and attacker behaviors.

- Improving Incident Response: By predicting where and how attacks are likely to occur, organizations can allocate resources more effectively, improving their incident response capabilities.

Despite its potential, the implementation of predictive analytics in cybersecurity faces several challenges:

- Data Quality and Quantity: The effectiveness of predictive analytics is heavily dependent on the quality and quantity of data. Inaccurate or incomplete data can lead to false predictions and missed threats.

- Algorithm Complexity: Designing and fine-tuning algorithms for predictive analytics is complex. There is a need for continuous adjustment and optimization to ensure accuracy.

- Interpretation of Results: The results of predictive analytics can sometimes be difficult to interpret, requiring skilled professionals who can understand and act on the insights provided.

- Privacy and Ethical Concerns: The collection and analysis of large volumes of data raise concerns regarding privacy and ethics, necessitating careful consideration of regulatory compliance and ethical standards.

Looking ahead, predictive analytics is set to play an increasingly central role in cybersecurity strategies. As machine learning and artificial intelligence technologies continue to advance, the capacity to predict and prevent cyber threats will become more refined and effective. The future of predictive analytics in cybersecurity points towards more autonomous, intelligent cybersecurity systems capable of not only defending against but also anticipating and adapting to the evolving cyber threat landscape.

Preparing for Future Cyber Threats

The first step in preparing for future cyber threats is understanding that the cyber landscape is in a constant state of flux. The threats that organizations face today may be vastly different from those they will encounter tomorrow. Emerging technologies such as artificial intelligence, the Internet of Things (IoT), and 5G networks, while bringing numerous benefits, also open new avenues for cyber attacks. Recognizing these changing dynamics is critical for effective preparation and response.

Moving from a reactive to a proactive defense strategy is essential in preparing for future threats. This involves not only safeguarding against known threats but also anticipating and preparing for potential future vulnerabilities.

- Risk Assessment and Analysis: Regularly assessing and analyzing potential risks and vulnerabilities is crucial. This includes keeping abreast of emerging cyber threats and understanding how they might impact existing systems and defenses.

- Investment in Advanced Technologies: Incorporating advanced technologies such as machine learning, predictive analytics, and automated defense systems can enhance the ability to detect and respond to sophisticated cyber threats.

- Red Team Exercises and Penetration Testing: Regularly conducting red team exercises and penetration testing can help organizations identify vulnerabilities and understand how an attacker might exploit their systems.

Enhancing Collaboration and Information Sharing

Collaboration and information sharing among organizations, cybersecurity experts, and governments can significantly strengthen collective defense against cyber threats.

- Partnerships and Alliances: Building partnerships and alliances with other organizations, cybersecurity firms, and government agencies can facilitate the sharing of threat intelligence and best practices.

- Participation in Cybersecurity Forums and Groups: Active participation in cybersecurity forums, working groups, and consortia can provide valuable insights and foster collaborative approaches to tackling emerging threats.

In the rapidly changing cybersecurity landscape, staying informed and being adaptive are key.

- Keeping Up with Technological Advancements: Organizations must keep up with technological advancements and understand how they can be leveraged to enhance cybersecurity or how they might introduce new vulnerabilities.

- Regulatory Compliance and Best Practices: Staying updated with the latest regulatory requirements and cybersecurity best practices is important for maintaining robust security measures.

Investing in Research and Development

Investment in research and development (R&D) in cybersecurity is crucial for staying ahead of cybercriminals.

- Innovative Security Solutions: Investing in the development of innovative security solutions can provide a competitive edge and enhance overall cybersecurity posture.

- Future-Proofing Security Measures: R&D can help in future-proofing security measures by anticipating and preparing for how emerging technologies might impact cybersecurity.

Afterword: Staying Updated in a Rapidly Evolving Field

In the dynamic realm of cybersecurity, staying updated is not just a recommendation; it's an imperative. The field is characterized by rapid developments, evolving threats, and continuously emerging technologies.

The first step to staying updated in cybersecurity is to recognize the nature and pace of change within the field. Cybersecurity is influenced by a range of factors including technological advancements, the evolving nature of threats, regulatory changes, and shifts in the digital landscape. This constant state of flux demands an approach to professional development that is proactive and adaptable.

Keeping abreast of industry trends is essential. This can be achieved through:

- Industry Publications and Journals: Regularly reading industry publications, journals, and whitepapers is a great way to stay informed about the latest research, trends, and developments.

- Online Resources and Blogs: Numerous online platforms, cybersecurity blogs, and forums provide up-to-date information on the latest cyber threats, defense strategies, and technological advancements.

- News and Media: Following reputable news sources and media outlets that focus on technology and cybersecurity can provide insights into the broader impacts of cybersecurity trends and events.

Practical Experience and Hands-On Learning

In cybersecurity, practical experience is as important as theoretical knowledge. Engaging in hands-on learning through real-world applications can greatly enhance understanding and skills. This includes:

- Simulations and Lab Work: Participating in simulations or lab work that mimic real-world cybersecurity scenarios can help in applying theoretical knowledge to practical situations.

- Hackathons and Competitions: Participating in hackathons and cybersecurity competitions is an excellent way to test and hone skills in a competitive and challenging environment.

Adaptability and curiosity are key traits for cybersecurity professionals. Embracing a culture of learning and being open to new ideas and approaches is essential. This involves being curious about new technologies, exploring different aspects of cybersecurity, and being willing to continually adapt and learn.

Finally, mentorship from experienced professionals can provide guidance and insights that are invaluable for professional growth. Similarly, collaborative learning experiences, such as group projects or team-based learning, can provide diverse perspectives and enhance understanding.

Best regards,

Liam Peterson

www.ingramcontent.com/pod-product-compliance
Lightning Source LLC
Chambersburg PA
CBHW031240050326
40690CB00007B/891